OFF AIR

OFF AIR

MY JOURNEY TO THE ANCHOR DESK

SHEBA TURK

FOREWORD BY SOLEDAD O'BRIEN

PELICAN PUBLISHING COMPANY
GRETNA 2018

*The word "Pelican" and the depiction of a pelican are
trademarks of Pelican Publishing Company, Inc., and are
registered in the U.S. Patent and Trademark Office.*

Library of Congress Cataloging-in-Publication Data

Names: Turk, Sheba author. | O'Brien, Soledad, 1966- author of foreword.
Title: Off air : my journey to the anchor desk / by Sheba Turk ; foreword by
Soledad O'Brien.
Description: Gretna : Pelican Publishing Company, 2018.
Identifiers: LCCN 2017059133| ISBN 9781455623914 (pbk. : alk. paper) | ISBN
9781455623921 (ebook)
Subjects: LCSH: Turk, Sheba. | Women television news anchors—United
States—Biography. | Television journalists—United States—Biography.
Classification: LCC PN4874.T85 A3 2018 | DDC 070.92 [B] —dc23 LC record
available at https://lccn.loc.gov/2017059133

Printed in the United States of America

Published by Pelican Publishing Company, Inc.
1000 Burmaster Street, Gretna, Louisiana 70053
www.pelicanpub.com

To my mom, for being my unwavering cheerleader and warrior

To my dad, for teaching me to work hard and laugh through it all

*To Polk, for being a partner who believes in
turning possibilities into our reality*

*To Kim, for adopting me as your own and
showing me that I really can do anything*

*To Soledad, for dragging me to the finish line so many times and supporting me
like one of your own*

*To Sally-Ann, for telling me to keep writing
even when the end seemed so far away*

To every viewer who has cheered for me from a distance

To every aspiring journalist, for inspiring me to share my story

To my family and friends

And, when you want something, all the universe conspires in helping you achieve it.

—Paulo Coelho, *The Alchemist*

Contents

Foreword

I travel all over the world to tell stories. I often meet people at their most vulnerable moments. Sometimes it's in the wake of a disaster, after an unimaginable loss, or as people are trying to recover from a devastating tragedy like Hurricane Katrina. I met so many young women in New Orleans, Louisiana, who lost everything in the storm. Many of these young women were missing the basics, such as reliable housing, and yet they had their sights set on a brighter future without the means to make that future their reality.

Sheba was one of those young women. I met her when she was getting close to graduating from college. It had been several years since Hurricane Katrina had destroyed her family's home. She was interested in journalism, and I invited her to come intern at CNN in New York with me. At the time, Sheba was going to college in New Orleans because she had run out of money to continue going to New York University. But she never talked much about her financial struggles.

In fact, I never looked at Sheba as someone who was struggling. She quickly stood out to my CNN team as someone who was reliable and smart, and she delivered results without any fuss. I grew up with parents who believed that at the end of the day, hard work wins and that if you were going to do something, do it well. Sheba operates with those same philosophies. She keeps her head down, puts in the effort, and lets her work speak for itself.

Sheba was living in my apartment in Manhattan while she was interning at CNN. I walked into the apartment one day and opened the refrigerator. There was a loaf of bread and a jar of peanut butter and nothing else. I thought to myself, "This girl is starving herself to be here." I understood then that she was willing to do whatever it took to be successful.

At the end of the summer, Sheba went back home to finish her senior year of college. My friend Kim was keeping an eye on Sheba down in New Orleans. Kim had been Sheba's college professor and introduced us. One day

Kim called to tell me that Sheba had run out of money for tuition again and was planning to drop out a second time. I didn't hesitate to write her a check. Like many young girls I have met, Sheba was willing to put in the effort to be successful, but she had some financial obstacles in her way. I had no doubt that if I removed that obstacle, Sheba would be successful.

That check allowed her to finish school. Sheba wasn't the only young woman who was struggling to graduate—and not because of grades or lack of effort, but from a lack of money. I started the PowHERful Foundation to help young women like Sheba finish school. For many young women, a check would mean the difference between dropping out of school and graduating.

While the check made a big difference, it still wasn't enough. Sheba had amazing parents who loved and supported her, but neither of Sheba's parents had finished college. So she had lots of questions for me about breaking into the professional world. She had questions about where she should look for her first job and how to prepare for her first interview, and the questions kept coming. The other young women I helped send to college needed more than money too. They needed career advice, relationship advice, a confidence boost, tips for managing stress, and many other things, depending on their circumstances. Money for tuition is a huge help, but they still need money for books, groceries, and laptops to help them get their work done. That's what my foundation provides. First off, we provide money for tuition and expenses, and then we make sure the girls have any other resources they need to succeed. Mentoring is a critical part of helping these young women reach their full potential. I think back to when I was beginning my career. I didn't understand that there was more to being successful than just doing my job. For instance, you need to know how to deal with people. There are so many unwritten rules of the office that I wish someone had told me when I was starting out. Unless you have someone in your corner who is invested in your future, no one is going to take the time to talk with you about those unwritten rules that can really help you progress in your career.

That's why Sheba's book is a great resource for aspiring journalists and, really, all young professionals. She talks about how mentoring and learning to speak up for herself helped her be successful in the news industry.

The most amazing thing about watching Sheba grow has been seeing her pay it forward. Sheba is now a mentor for my foundation. We partnered her with a young woman named Tassion, who is attending Dillard University in New Orleans and who also has an interest in journalism. Sheba takes her role as Tassion's mentor very seriously, and she is always looking for new ways to pass along all that she is learning to the young ladies coming behind her. And that is all I want from the young women my foundation sends to school. Sheba shares her story with the thousands of young women who attend PowHERful conferences around the country. We spend a day talking to young women about how to prepare for their futures. This book is just another extension of Sheba's efforts to pass along her knowledge to other young women.

When I met Sheba, she was dreaming of following in my footsteps and being a journalist, and now she is on her way to a promising future. She works as a morning anchor in New Orleans at WWL-TV and hosts her own entertainment show. I see how young girls are looking up to her now, and I know that they don't know all that she went through to get to where she is. It's interesting that Sheba and I both started off college pre-med, with no intention of working in journalism. I started working at a TV station for internship credit when I was an undergraduate at Harvard. I loved it, and I was good at it. But there was nothing fabulous about the day-to-day work in the beginning of my career, which is just fine. I think it is so important that Sheba stresses that in this book. In my early days in the news business, I was grabbing coffee and running errands. Success is not about being glamorous. It is about doing the work.

When I was just beginning my career on TV and was doing my first live shot in San Francisco, a man pinched me on the butt right as I went live. I was caught so off guard that I couldn't gather myself. It was terrible and many people suggested that I quit. Instead, I focused on what I could control and made lists of things I needed to do to get better, and I did. Eventually, I became a bureau chief. When people see me on TV now, they would never think that someone who needed so much work back then could come so far.

Sheba has come a long way too. Mainly because she understands that the road to success isn't always easy. She lived off peanut butter sandwiches for weeks during her CNN internship because she understands that it will take sacrifice to reach your goals. It wasn't until very recently that Sheba asked me why I chose to help her out of all the young women I had come across who needed help. It's because she is so positive. She had more than enough reasons to give up or complain or just have a terrible attitude about her situation. Instead, she was the complete opposite. She was focused on what she could do to keep moving forward, instead of dwelling on things that were out of her control.

And that's a great mind-set to have in the news business. When you're on air in seven minutes and your live interview cancels on you, you have to have

Sheba's mind-set: "OK. What can I do to make it work?" I am a mom of four and the CEO of my own production company, so I have to be flexible because something is always going off plan. My mom always said, "When things go wrong, you get one day to cry, sob, and do nothing but feel absolutely miserable about yourself. And then the next day, start moving forward." I don't believe in excuses. I think that most problems are very fixable. Sometimes that requires someone stepping in to help. And in this book, Sheba shows that she is constantly working on forward progress. Every time I have given Sheba an assignment or brought her on a project with me, she has come in and delivered. When things are not going as planned, instead of freaking out, she does what successful people do. She smiles and makes it work.

I am glad she is sharing her journey here because hopefully it will inspire other young people to realize that a great attitude can really make you stand out and set you on a path to success. They need to see someone who chooses to keep moving forward despite obstacles, because it works. Sheba's viewers and social media followers see the bright, shiny version of her story, but behind the camera, the real Sheba has a story that many people can take something from. And I am happy to be a part of it.

Soledad O'Brien
Journalist, CEO of Starfish Media Group,
and founder of the PowHERful Foundation

Introduction

I could be the poster child for a campaign on quitting. There's this myth that quitting is for losers, but I love quitting. I love a good "I'm done. I'm moving on. I don't have to deal with that anymore." In fact, I got where I am today because I quit many times along the way. I had a major breakthrough in college when I quit the pre-med track and decided to follow my passion for writing. That's when I realized how much I loved quitting. I felt free. I was happier. I could redirect my energy to classes that were a better fit for me. Because I quit pre-med and started considering journalism, I found my way to WWL-TV. It was around March 2011 when I got the quitting itch again. I was a recent college graduate and had been working at WWL, the New Orleans CBS affiliate, for about seven months. I was a part-time associate producer, which basically means being a writer for the morning news, but the job wasn't exactly what I wanted.

It would have been easier to walk away if I hated my job. I didn't hate it. I just really wanted to be a reporter. I could have kept my position as an associate producer and continued on a path to becoming a full-time producer, but that would have been the easy road for me, since I was already on that track. I wanted to take a risk and make the leap to reporting, but I was apprehensive. My managers kept telling me that I would make a great producer. What if I wouldn't do as good a job reporting? What if no one wanted to hire me? What if the only job I could get was in some small town that I didn't want to work in? I wanted to quit, but there were so many unknowns. And I knew people would think I was crazy for walking away from WWL. It's a legacy station that has been number one in New Orleans for decades. And who was I to quit anywhere? Yes, I was making only ten dollars an hour, but I had a job. And it was in my desired field. After running out of money for college twice and struggling financially my entire life, I should have just been happy to have any job, right? Wrong. None of it was good enough.

Come to think of it, I have always been a person who is either fully dedicated to something and giving it my all or ready to walk away and completely leave it alone. I went to kindergarten in an area of New Orleans known as the Seventh Ward. The school was called Martinez, and every year, there were these epic end-of-the-year productions. Each student would raise money, and the highest fundraisers would get a position in our school's version of a royal court. There was a king and queen, and a ton of other made-up positions. I was the "sweetheart" one year and, at five years old in a large auditorium, sang "A Whole New World" from *Aladdin* in a rendition that my mother will claim was Grammy-worthy. Let's just not ask anyone else for a review. When I was four, I was crowned the "flower girl"—literally, with a crown of flowers. We practiced for weeks, rehearsing the songs, choreography, and things we had to say during the performance. My parents shelled out money for a beautiful white dress. I went to the hairdresser to get Shirley Temple curls, which were reserved for special occasions. I was all into it until the day of the big event. My older brother, I think, had an end-of-the-school-year ceremony that day too. I remember we had run around a lot that day and four-year-old Sheba was tired and not having it. My mom dressed me like a doll, and I went in there acting like a doll, all right. The problem was, it was Chucky! I refused to wear the flower crown, which was, apparently, mandatory for the flower girl. I just plain old cut up. It's one of my earliest memories, and I don't know why it sticks with me.

Besides that, I hardly ever gave my parents any problems. The details are fuzzy, but we made it through the evening without my cooperation. I don't even remember my mom being mad. There was no spanking. In fact, I was never spanked growing up—no screaming, no punishment at all. Instead, the next day, she kept me home from school, bought some Popeyes chicken, and took me for a picnic in the park. And while we ate, she talked to four-year-old Sheba like she talks to adult Sheba. She explained that if I wanted to do something, I had to be all in. I had to be prepared to do it all the way through without acting a fool, or I could decide that I didn't want to do it at all.

And that was just it. My heart just wasn't 100 percent into being an associate producer. Be totally committed or don't do it at all. That was the mind-set I had with everything: school, professional opportunities, relationships. I would have never found what or who I truly love if I would not have quit the things that just weren't for me. I have had to quit people who shouldn't have been in my life, jobs that weren't moving me closer to my future goals, and many other things that proved to be distractions from achieving my dreams. The more I thought about my future, the more I realized that quitting wasn't just for losers. By hanging in there, I was losing. I was losing time and energy—which I could have been spending on my ultimate vision—on something that I wasn't passionate about.

And the ultimate vision was to be successful and happy. The key word there is "and." After being at WWL for a few months, I noticed that having a certain position or salary didn't automatically bring success or happiness. I always imagined that everyone who worked at certain companies or had big, fancy jobs must be happy. Then I discovered what I call "the happiness myth." I realized there are people with jobs others would kill to have who are not happy. It seemed to me many of these people had settled and taken the easy road instead of taking risks. I didn't want that to be me.

My mom always says that everything is twenty-twenty in hindsight. And through the process of writing this book, I know how true those words are. It is easy to talk about my journey to the anchor desk now because I know how things turn out. I can look back and see how my choices were helping me move forward, but at the time, I was flying blind. I felt lost when deciding on a career plan in college. Working in the news industry was never part of my plan. I refused to even watch the news when I was growing up. I just wasn't interested. I didn't develop an appreciation for journalism until I was sixteen years old. That's when Hurricane Katrina devastated New Orleans and took me away from the only place I knew as home. Even then, working in the news never crossed my mind. Growing up, I wanted to be a veterinarian, then a dolphin trainer, then an anthropologist. At one point, I just wanted to make collages. I was all over the place. I was more than halfway through college before it ever even occurred to me to consider journalism as a career option.

Just when I started becoming clearer about my future goals, I was spinning out of control again. I ran out of money for college twice and even had to drop out for a semester for financial reasons. I did eventually graduate but not without a lot of support. I have amazing parents, who sacrificed so much to put me on a path to success, but neither of my parents finished college. So when it came to the career side of things, I never had anyone to look up to. That's where Kim Bondy came in. She was one of my college professors and has worked in practically all aspects of the business, including as a former CNN executive. She introduced me to her best friend, the award-winning journalist Soledad O'Brien, who also became my mentor, and who would eventually step in to make sure that I could graduate from college. When I started looking for jobs, none of the out-of-town stations I applied to would hire me. I felt as though I was constantly being detoured from the great future

I wanted for myself. I know now I was being detoured onto the right path. The key to my progress has been moving forward despite a million things going wrong. Even I couldn't have imagined that I would be promoted four times in just two years at WWL, making my way from associate producer, to traffic reporter, to morning show field reporter, to anchor.

Life is not a movie. There was never a big light bulb that went off in my head before a big decision. Every time I sat around waiting for one, I realized that I was stagnant when I could have been making small steps forward. I certainly did not have a glorious epiphany the moment I decided to finally start pursuing reporting jobs seriously. I still had a lot of doubt about my abilities as a reporter, but what I knew for certain was that I did not like the look of my future as an associate producer. I didn't realize how much of a game changer talking to the news director would be. I just followed my gut. Something inside me kept saying, "Don't settle." I was making an epic leap, but in the moment, it felt as if I was barely crawling forward. Viewers have watched my pursuit of success through the TV screen, rooting me on as I made my way to the anchor desk, but most people don't really know how my off-air story unfolded. I am sharing that journey here so that those coming behind me can see what it takes to move up the ladder and understand what it's like to work in the news industry when the cameras are not on. This is what the pursuit of success looks like off air. For me, it all began when I went to the news director's office and told him that I was going to quit my job at WWL.

Career Timeline

May 2011

Graduated from the University of New Orleans

September 2011

Hired by WWL-TV as an associate producer

May 2012

Promoted to WWL traffic reporter

April 2013

Promoted to morning show field reporter

August 2013

Hosted the first episode of *The 504*

October 2013

Promoted to co-anchor of *Eyewitness Morning News*

OFF AIR

Season's Greetings '97

At six years old, with Santa Claus. (Photograph by Fred Parker & Dennis Photo Finish, Ltd.)

1

Throwing It All the Way Back

It isn't where you came from; it's where you're going that counts.

Ella Fitzgerald

My Family

Being successful was never an option for me. I was raised to believe that if I stayed focused and worked hard, the possibilities were endless. Thankfully, ignorance was bliss. I did not realize that the odds were not in my favor. I grew up in the Seventh Ward of New Orleans, in a house on the corner of Touro and Hope Streets on a block that was once a nice area but was becoming filled with more crime and drug activity as I grew older. My mom stopped working when my older brother was born, two years before I came along. She had started college right out of high school, but by the time she had her first child at nearly thirty, she hadn't finished yet and put that goal to the side. She had spent time doing everything from teaching to office work. My dad didn't go to college at all. He started working on trains for Amtrak at just twenty-two years old. Even though they didn't finish college, my parents valued education more than anything for their children.

I was obsessed with school from as early as I can remember. My mom enrolled me in a pre-kindergarten (pre-K) program to give me a head start in the classroom, so that I would be more than prepared for kindergarten. I complained because the pre-K teachers did not assign students homework as the kindergarten teachers did. My older brother was doing homework, so I wanted some too. My mom moved me to another school that assigned homework. Turns out, my love for academics wasn't just a childish obsession. I loved school even as I got older.

My dad earned a modest income, and my mom was busy doing everything for her children. My baby brother came as a surprise five years after me. My mom and dad could not have been more attentive, nurturing, and loving toward their children, but as time went on, money became tighter and tighter. It was causing tension.

Studying was my solace. I would immerse myself in schoolwork or a novel to mentally escape everything going on at home. It's funny how the exact same environment produces different effects in different people. My older brother grew less interested in school as we got older, getting by with the least amount of effort. He found his love in music. We were both in the band in elementary school. I was pretending to play the keyboard, and he was becoming a whiz on the drums.

Just as things were becoming more strained inside our home, things continued going downhill around us. By the time I was in elementary school, most of the young guys in the neighborhood had become involved with drugs and were always lurking on the streets. One neighbor had two terrible sons around my age who grew up to be the neighborhood menaces. I remember running to get my mom when they jumped our fence and destroyed our play set.

People usually don't believe me when I tell them where I grew up. They say I don't sound like someone from that area. I was so sheltered that my neighborhood didn't have much of an influence on me. My mom allowed me to hang out with only one girl, who lived around the corner in our neighborhood. My parents couldn't afford to move, so my mom kept us inside to shield us from everything that was going on around us. No matter how bad things were financially, my mom insisted we go to private schools, even for pre-K. In New Orleans, the public school system was struggling. With low graduation rates and test scores, many public school students in the city couldn't compete on a national level.

School was a different world from our neighborhood. I started developing two different voices without even noticing it. At home, I still spoke as my family did. Calling the sink a "zink," as many New Orleanians do, and eliminating verbs from sentences occasionally, "Where he at?" Eventually, however, my mom noticed that I was starting to speak as the people I was around at school all day did:

"Did you have a good day?" she would always ask when she picked me up from school.

"Yah, we had chicken nuggets and mashed potatoes for lunch—" but before I could finish, she would call me out.

"Since when did you start saying 'yah'? That's what Valley girls say. We say 'yeah,'" she reminded me.

I would continue to fill her in on my day, but she would always interrupt my story to correct me. Those two different voices stuck with me into adulthood.

My friends are used to me switching back and forth. When I'm around new people, they usually mention that sometimes I sound "really New Orleans" and other times I don't. It is a constant reminder that I have always felt as if I were juggling two different worlds.

As for my family's finances, we were operating on a wing and prayer, as my mom likes to say. Our financial situation made me feel a little bit like an outsider at school. My parents were living paycheck to paycheck. We often didn't have money to go out to eat after soccer games. If the car broke, it might be months before it was fixed. To be clear, my dad made a decent salary, but there were other factors playing a role in my parents' mismanagement of money. I will tell that part of the story one day later in life, when I feel the time is right. I don't want to paint a picture that shows my brothers and I always being deprived. That would be far from the truth. When my parents got money, they spent it on things for us, even when they couldn't afford to. I had a collection of American Girl dolls. They were one hundred dollars a piece. Yes, one hundred dollars for a doll. I had five or six by the time I was a teenager. And then, some days, my parents could barely scrape together lunch money for us.

Our finances being a mess impacted more than just what we could or could not buy. My brothers and I were often invited to our classmates' homes, but we could never have our friends from school over to our house. My mom didn't want us playing around in that neighborhood, so she certainly didn't feel right having other parents drop their kids off there. Plus, things were always such a mess inside. There was clothing and junk everywhere. Our home reflected the chaos that my parents were dealing with internally. My elementary school would hold my report card at the end of the year until my parents could pay the tuition balance. The first time this happened, I was very upset. My mom helped me understand that in the large scheme of things, it wasn't a big deal. I knew that I had straight As and that they would get my report card as soon as they could.

My mom would substitute teach and pick up odd jobs now and then, but she was determined to be there for us. She wanted to be able to pick us up from school and attend all of the activities in which we were involved. My dad worked on the train. His routes shifted throughout the years. When I was young, he'd travel back and forth to Florida, then to Chicago, and finally to New York. His schedule varied with the routes; he always worked several days out of town and came back for a few days in between trips. One of the great perks of his job was that we got to travel for free on the train, and since my dad was working, he had a hotel room wherever he was going. I went to Chicago and New York numerous times as a child. The trips were quick. Sometimes, we were in the city for less than twenty-four hours. It didn't take me long to fall in love with New York, though—the tall buildings, everyone moving fast, the bagels!

The downside of my dad's schedule was that my mom was the only one who could regularly pick us up from school and keep up with our schedules. Things were chaotic enough. She didn't want to get a regular nine-to-five and leave us figuring out how to get home on our own. We also had a lot going on outside of class. My brother was part of the band and played basketball. I played soccer and volleyball and was in the ceramics club (cool kid alert). I wanted to enroll in gymnastics or try ballet, but my mom said that we couldn't afford those classes. She knew that if she got a job, it would prevent us from doing all of the school activities we could. And she was the one who sacrificed the most for her decision. I can barely remember my mom ever buying things for herself. When I was really young, she would get her hair done or buy a new outfit occasionally, but as the money grew tighter, she gave all of that up for us. My parents bought a nice used SUV, but with hardly any money for maintenance, it fell apart over the years. One of the windows broke one day. My mom closed it up with garbage bags and duct tape, and it stayed liked that for years.

Finding Stability

We were all riding in the car. There was a dip in the interstate as we drove up the slope of the bridge. We couldn't see what was on the other side. We kept going, and suddenly I realized the bridge would just end. There was nothing but water. I was frozen with terror, and the car flew in the air, heading into the water.

Then, I woke up. I had that dream more times in my childhood than I can count. It wasn't until I got into my late teens that I became curious about the meaning of this recurring nightmare. I did some research and found that dreams about being a passenger in a car driving off of a bridge symbolized a lack of control. That made perfect sense. There were many things going on around me that I couldn't control, especially my family's finances. But part of my motivation to excel academically was a belief that by working hard, I could call the shots one day. Only now can I see that in many of those moments where I felt I was spinning out of control, I was actually being turned in the direction I needed to go. It amazes me now to think that if I had been in complete control, I wouldn't be where I am, because I could not have possibly planned for things to be as good as they are.

Over the years, I made steps toward being in control of my life. Nothing gave me more power than my education. In the classroom, I was in control. I could study as hard as I wanted to, and I could control the outcomes of my tests. At school, if I did the work, things could be perfect. My mom taught me to do my best, accept whatever that was, and not compare myself to others. Even though I always had straight As (except for second grade, when I missed a lot of school because of allergies), my mom would have been happy if I had brought home Cs, as long as I promised her it was the best I could do. My mom told me not to worry about anything going on at home. She always said doing well in school would make things different for me in the future.

Around fourth or fifth grade, I stopped speaking in class entirely when the bell rang to begin class, and I wouldn't open my mouth to another student until the bell rang for class to end. At my elementary school, we had behavior cards that we had to flip over if the teacher caught us doing anything against the rules throughout the day, such as not doing our work, passing notes, or talking in class. I decided that I didn't want my card turned over—ever. When the bell rang, I was silent. No "God bless you" for sneezes. If a friend missed something the teacher said and leaned over to ask me, I would point or write it down. It was strange, I know. My classmates made a game out of it. They would try to get me to talk. When I run into them now, they still mention how quiet I was. Anyone who really knows me knows I have a hard time shutting up. The silence in class was just another way for me to create this perfect life at school to make up for the imperfect parts of my home life. I was a very happy child. It wasn't until I got older that I was able to look back and see how my home life affected me. My mom always taught me to be myself, so I was OK feeling different. I was popular and well liked. I was the cool, smart kid. The quiet thing came off as funny. My phone would ring off the hook before exams, with my classmates trying to get help before our tests. I fit in, in my own weird way.

As I approached my high school years, my parents still insisted on putting me in pricey Catholic schools. I would get called to the office over the intercom and get sent home when my parents were behind on tuition. I became used to it, because it happened several times. Sometimes, my parents would warn me in the morning that they were behind on tuition. Other times, there was no warning at all. But I loved school, and I could see how hard things were for my parents. So I was grateful, even though the road was rocky. I don't support making bad financial decisions—now that I know better—but thank God my parents put my education first. I always looked forward to the day when our money issues would be a thing of the past. My parents sacrificed so much for my education that it made me take school even more seriously.

When things didn't go as planned, my mom always said not to worry because everything happens for a reason. Besides, she did enough worrying for all of us. When I was in high school, my mom really wanted to move out of the neighborhood, but we still couldn't afford it. One night, my brother said that his PlayStation was gone. As we started looking around, we noticed other stuff was gone too: TVs, more games. We had been robbed. The burglar probably didn't have to work too hard to enter. Our front door had broken, and my dad had propped it back up by piling stuff behind it. People were always just standing around outside, so someone in the neighborhood had probably noticed that there was an easy entrance. We couldn't afford to fix the door, so it stayed like that. Another time, I heard what we all thought was a car backfiring, only to learn it was a shooting. My parents knew the guy who did the shooting. He was one of the regular faces in the neighborhood. Not long after that, we lost our house. The door was never fixed, so before we could move, we were robbed again. My parents had tried as hard as possible to keep the money struggles from affecting their children. They explained to us that the house had foreclosed, and by then, we had to be out in a few days.

It was a chaotic move. My mom had found us a new house to rent in a nice

My family (left to right): my younger brother, Jaron; my older brother, Jye; my boyfriend; my mom; and my dad. (Photograph taken with author's cell phone [hereafter, "by author"])

My mom, 2017. (Photograph by author)

area of the Gentilly neighborhood. We had three dogs. We were back and forth between the two houses for a few days, so we left the dogs at the old house. We came back to find all of the dogs had been let out of the yard. Two of the dogs came right back after we called for them. My little brother had a black Lab that was known to bark and growl at anyone who passed, and he was nowhere to be found. One of our neighbors heard us looking for the dog and told us two boys had jumped the fence earlier that day to attack him. She said he had gotten out through the fence and went running down the street, but the boys chased after him. It was nighttime, but we drove around calling for him. We never found him.

It didn't take long to realize that foreclosure was a blessing. This is how many blessings would enter my life. Things would be an absolute mess. I'd hit rock bottom, with no sign of opportunity. I'd hold on tight and ride the waves. The same waves that made me feel out of control and beaten down would push me in a better direction.

Our new neighborhood was so peaceful. There weren't groups of guys aimlessly hanging around on the street all day and night. I felt safe for the first time in years. Situations like that, where I was completely not in control, are part of the reason nothing keeps me down too long. I have seen time and time again that life will always deliver the unexpected. But nothing productive came out of dwelling on those things. Sometimes those unexpected moments changed things for the better in the long run. I would get kicked out of school but jump right back in as if nothing happened and work harder. After we lost our home, we moved to another and kept pushing forward. There was always some hurdle to jump over, but I followed my parents' lead. Jump and keep it moving.

It worked. Education and my parents helped me thrive despite my surroundings. Through everything, my parents were open with me about their mistakes and set the path for me to do better. I am who I am because of the values my parents instilled in me. My mom continues to show me what unconditional love and sacrifice really mean. She provided the best for her children, even when it meant the worst for her. She was frustrated by her situation, but quitting was never an option. When it came to her own schooling, she would drop out for all kinds of reasons, but she always went back. I follow her example to this day. I don't react to many things others see as obstacles or problems, because I'd rather spend that energy moving forward. My mother's idealistic nature wore off on me in a way that I now see as key to my success. I never pitied myself or wished for anyone else's life. I merely noted they were different.

My dad is the funniest person I know. My mom would scold him in church for making me laugh when everyone was supposed to be quiet. I have always thought of him as my mom's fourth child. He has a gift that allows him to find the humor in everything. He passed that on to me. A shift in perspective can turn even tragedy into another reason to smile. He's extremely dedicated to his job and takes pride in exceeding expectations at work.

My parents prove that being amazing parents is not about being perfect. They sacrificed to shield their children from all of the crazy going on. And it worked because despite everything, I really believed that I could do whatever I wanted with my life. If I would have been asked back then to talk about obstacles, I genuinely would have said that I didn't have any to talk about. They showed me that money was not the key to happiness and that if I stayed focused on my education, I could have the life I wanted one day. I don't know where I would be without my mom and dad. I am grateful to have always felt loved and supported. They laid the foundation for me to be where I am today.

Hurricane Katrina

My parents supported my education at St. Mary's Dominican High School, a Catholic all-girl school that several of my friends from elementary school attended. In New Orleans, it's not odd to attend an all-girl or all-boy high school. My best friends to this day are some of the girls who walked the halls with me every day at Dominican. Most of them I had known long before then. My best friend and I still joke about the time her Barbie Jeep broke down in the Mardi Gras school parade in first grade, and I was right there for her to hop into mine. We kept the good times going at Dominican and were ready to make more memories together as we headed back to school in August 2005 to begin our junior year. We were reunited for about a week when we found out we'd have a few days off because a hurricane was coming.

Like everyone else in New Orleans, we were used to the threat of a storm and figured we'd be back in school the following week. My family wasn't planning to leave the city because of car issues. Our relatives had called all day the Saturday before the storm hit, asking if we were going to Houston to stay with family there for a few days until the storm blew over. My mom finally decided to leave after one of my cousins called around nine that Saturday night before the storm hit. At the time, my parents were driving an old minivan. It was white with two black doors—hence, its nickname "The Skunk." It had been a taxicab before my parents bought it, and someone did a terrible job of scratching off the company logo. It ran about as good as it looked. If things took a turn for the worst at the last minute, my mom knew that the van was not reliable and we could possibly be stuck without a way to leave the city. So we left the minivan behind and piled into my relatives' cars. My mom, my dad, my younger brother (who was ten at the time), my dad's mom, my aunts, and a few of my cousins squeezed into three cars and took off.

I was sixteen then, and since, so many details have started to fade. How long did it take to get to Houston? I just remember lots of traffic and hearing my family say it was taking much longer than it usually would to get there. Who did I sit next to in the car? In what hotel did we stay at first? The timing of everything is fuzzy too. Did we stay at the hotel for a day or a week, before moving on to my cousin's house? How long was it before we came back to New Orleans? At the time, I thought I would remember forever every moment of that year in Texas.

There are several moments from the experience that continue to smolder in my memory and still burn if I get too close. I was filling up the bathtub with water for my dog, Sandy, just before we left. I remember thinking that I didn't want him to run out of water if we were gone for more than two days. I'd had him for seven years. He was a large Catahoula-hound mix. The car was full, and it wasn't ours, so we left him. I quickly told him goodbye before we piled into the car. I would have never left him if I had known it would be the last time I'd ever see him.

My family is one that laughs through the good times and bad. We made fun of my aunt for filling her car with what looked like her entire house. Her computer, clothes, and small pieces of furniture could all be seen through the back window of her car. She was the only one who wouldn't end up regretting what she left behind.

After two or so days in a hotel, it was clear that we wouldn't be going home soon. I still hadn't grasped how bad things were. When one of my relatives said we might never be able to go back, it sank in that the unimaginable had happened. Most of New Orleans was inundated with water. We left the hotel for my cousin's modest home, which she shared with her four kids. She took in us and more than a dozen other relatives. We slept on the bed, on the floor, or on the couch for months.

Service to cell phones with New Orleans area codes was down, so it was hard to find out if the relatives who had gone other ways were OK. At some point, we learned that my grandmother who had schizophrenia had been left behind by her caretaker. We had no idea where she was and spent hours a day online looking for postings of her. No one had heard from one of my uncles either. For a few long weeks, we spent our days looking for my grandmother on websites where people had posted those who were missing and websites where people looked for their relatives. I don't remember anymore how long it took to find them, but after a few weeks, all of my family and friends were accounted for and, thankfully, safe.

I spent several hours a day looking through postings of dogs that had been rescued and relocated to shelters across the country. I found several that I wanted to believe were my dog, only to have my mom point out obvious features that were different, such as the wrong paw color or ear shape. We had heard that Gentilly, where we lived, was one of the hardest hit areas, but we weren't certain about our house. I remember watching video of an area about a mile from our house. I had hoped the coverage would go further so that I could see that my dog was OK, but it stopped. The water was too deep for the camera crews to go any further.

We didn't know until weeks later, but we had lost everything, including my dog. I have never felt so desperately hopeful as I felt when I prayed for my dog to be alive. To this day, I remember pleading with God to let me have one thing, my dog. Please let him have been rescued. I had accepted that everything was gone, but I was okay because I had convinced myself that somehow my dog had been saved. And in my sixteen-year-old mind, finding out that he was gone made everything collapse, as it already had for so many who had swam through the floodwaters back in New Orleans, been trapped inside their homes, or lost people they loved.

My parents returned to the city as soon as they could to see what was left. I think it was mid-September by then. I am allergic to mold, so I stayed in a hotel with my little brother while they salvaged what they could. I begged my parents to let me walk into the house just for a second. I had to see for myself. Everything was out of place, covered in mold, and sat quietly in a new place, as though this chaotic mess was the new normal. I can still see the hole cut in the bathroom door. The door had swollen through the frame. That's where we had left my dog.

My mom was a warrior through it all, as she always is. But between trying to find my grandmother and uncle, figuring out where we would live, and managing things without a car—since we'd left ours in New Orleans—she never enrolled my brother and me in school. At the end of October, the rest of my friends were in school somewhere, but we were just settling in, in Texas. We had moved from my cousin's house to a hotel room, where I lived with my mom, dad, and brother for a month. We finally found a house in Katy, just outside of Houston. My parents used some of the disaster assistance money from the Federal Emergency Management Agency (FEMA) to get a car. We finally had a way to get to school, but the first semester was almost over.

Somehow, my mom enrolled us in schools in Katy, and the schools worked with us to get caught up. I ended up at Katy High School. When the Texas public school students learned that I had gone to a Catholic school back home, they thought I was a nun. Aside from that slight misunderstanding, I met so many nice people. I will never forget the new friends who accepted me from day one and the teachers and counselors who worked with me and saw me through my junior year. But even with the warm welcome, it wasn't home. I missed my friends and Dominican. Not long after going back to school, I started getting sick. I was always nauseous and didn't want to eat. I kept going to the doctor to try new medicines. The doctor told me it was stress, but I insisted something was wrong.

After a year in Texas, we moved back to New Orleans so that I could finish my senior year of high school at Dominican. The return was hard. Things had been better for my family in Texas. "Katrina" has become synonymous with "devastation," so it's hard to explain to people that, financially, the hurricane actually helped my family. First, there was all kinds of assistance for storm victims. My mom went through a long battle with FEMA to get money for everything we lost. We didn't have flood insurance, so there would have been no other compensation for our belongings. We also had food stamps, even though we wouldn't have qualified under normal circumstances. But FEMA's Disaster Supplemental Nutrition Assistance Program (D-SNAP) was offering short-term food relief to families affected by Katrina.

My parents found a home to rent, and it was bigger and nicer—and in a quieter neighborhood—than anything we could have afforded in New Orleans. The owner even discussed setting up a plan to sell it to them. My family made friends with our neighbors. We were going to public school, which was free, but I wasn't happy. I told my mom I wanted to graduate from Dominican, and she made it happen. In New Orleans, we couldn't find anywhere affordable to live. My mom, dad, and brother moved into a trailer on a friend's property in the Seventh Ward, and I moved in with another Dominican classmate in Gentilly. I will be forever grateful to my family for passing up great opportunities for something that meant so much to me.

Hurricane Katrina and the Media

After Katrina hit, I couldn't get enough of the news. It was the first time I had ever cared about anything on the news. National media outlets were showing the devastation, and I couldn't tear my eyes away from the TV. The grocery stores, neighborhoods—everything that was familiar to me was surrounded by water.

We were being referred to as "refugees" on the news. I was offended. It felt as if we were being painted as wild outsiders in our own country. We were victims, we were displaced, and many of us had lost everything. But we were not refugees. Katrina shaped the way I deliver the news today. The last thing I want to do is offend a person in a story I am covering. When I am on a scene or telling a story, I think about what I would want to know or how I would want to be referred to if a story personally affected me.

My goal is to tell every story as though it is the "Katrina" of someone else's life. A life lost to violence or a house lost to fire can be just another sad story on the news for many of us, but for someone else, it may be the moment that pushes them down a path to a long, painful journey.

Katrina was empowering in a sense. Losing so much and being able to move on made me feel as if nothing could ever defeat me. The experience stripped away so much that it was easy to identify what really mattered, and that was my family. A girl I had gone to elementary school with in New Orleans ended up being at the same school as me in Texas. When someone asked us what we brought with us from home, she said she had gone back for all of her clothes because she couldn't imagine living without them. I didn't have to imagine living without mine anymore. I was doing it. Childhood pictures, clothes, my TV, my bed, my books, and those expensive American Girl dolls— all gone. And, of course, we had no insurance coverage on any of our personal items. That moment was one of the first times it clicked for me: Many of the things that were hard for me now would make me stronger in the long run. I was never a materialistic person. There were certainly things I wanted, but whether I had them or not didn't affect my happiness. Katrina showed me how fleeting material things can be. It was comforting to know that I don't need much to be happy. I still had my family. The rest was negotiable.

2

Decisions, Decisions, Decisions

*You don't have to see the whole staircase, just take the
first step.*

Dr. Martin Luther King, Jr.

Leaving New Orleans

Hurricane Katrina changed my life in many ways. The aftermath of the
storm played a big role in my decision to leave New Orleans for college. The
year my family spent in Texas was the only extended amount of time that I
had spent outside of New Orleans. We took family vacations and lots of short
trips on the train, but we had never stayed long enough for me to compare
the city to New Orleans. New Orleans is odd in many ways. I had no idea that
public school was normal. I thought the norm was the way things were in New
Orleans. Many of our public schools were not preparing students adequately
to succeed, and parents had to pay for schooling to guarantee their kids got
a decent education. In Texas, there was no such thing as being in an upscale
neighborhood and then, two blocks later, being in an area that was filled with
houses that weren't kept up and had men lingering on the corner. Oh, and I
was also shocked that streets in Texas were not filled with potholes, as they
are in New Orleans.

Don't get me wrong. I love New Orleans. But after living in Texas, I felt
betrayed by the place I had always known as home. New Orleans could do a
better job of caring for the people who live there. If you have money, you can
love wherever you go, because you will have the best of it. The baffling thing
about the Katrina aftermath is that people who lived in some of the poorest,
most crime-ridden areas were clawing to get back after Katrina sent them
elsewhere. Wherever they had landed didn't feel like home. I knew exactly
what they were going through.

We have had a massive influx of newcomers to the city since Katrina. It
seems the city is catering to outsiders as opposed to the loyal people who

chose to return to this city with nothing. Many people who live in the city don't make wages high enough to afford the rising cost of housing. The education system is not where it should be, and violent crime is a major issue. Katrina opened my eyes to the fact that people in other parts of the country had different opportunities than we did. Though I loved New Orleans, this realization made me want to leave home and see what else was in store.

In-State versus Out-of-State

I returned to Dominican for all of our senior year festivities. I let out a sigh of relief at our senior class ring ceremony. My older brother was still off at college. My parents and little brother were living in a friend's trailer in an area that was devastated by the storm. I was living with one of my friends. Our situation was "all hooked up," but at least we were finally back home. As someone discussed how hard the year had been, my best friend, who is not very emotional, cried. She had also been gone our entire junior year. We remained friends during that time by spending countless hours video-chatting online. When we were on the phone just joking around, it was almost as if we were back home. Now, we actually were. Just like that, my stomach issues went away. I guess the doctor had been right about me being stressed.

Before we knew it, it was time to start applying for colleges. I had always thought I was going to stay in New Orleans or go to school close by. I hadn't gone on any college tours as my friends had before the storm. The friend I was living with submitted applications online to several colleges all across the country. She knew that I loved going to New York and told me that I should apply to New York University (NYU) with her. The only thing I knew about the university was that it was in Manhattan. I thought about how great it would be to get away from New Orleans again once I finished school, and I did love New York. I was sold. I told my parents about the plan. My mom was not too happy about me wanting to go away, but she gave me the money I needed for the application. After submitting, I didn't give the NYU application or any of the others much consideration. I was sure that I would get into Louisiana State University (LSU), which is where my brother went and probably where I would go too. My friend and I spent the next few months applying to any scholarships we could find online.

The acceptance letters didn't come for months. By then, my parents had found a home to rent, and we were all living together again. The friend who I had been living with let me know that she had gotten a rejection letter from NYU. I was sure mine would come soon. She had taken Advanced Placement classes, and I hadn't. I had wanted to enroll in them in my senior year, but I wasn't able to complete the prerequisites while I was in Texas. And she was involved in more school activities. A few days went by, and I got an acceptance letter and a scholarship for half of my tuition. I don't know if I had even thought about tuition before then. The moment NYU became an option, I started fantasizing about living in New York and going to school there, even though I had also gotten accepted to all of the other local colleges I had applied to.

Paying for College

There was only one problem with my fantasy: Reality! NYU cost $60,000 a year. Even with the half-tuition scholarship, it was too much money. I started preparing to attend LSU. I accepted the offer, picked out my dorm room, and started emailing my roommates. But my mom knew that if money had not been an issue, I would have gone to NYU. So she ignored all of my plans for LSU, and even though she didn't want to see me go, she started talking to my dad to figure out how to get me to New York.

My parents were expecting to receive some money from my grandmother's recent passing, and my dad was getting a promotion at work. Without doing any real math, they decided that the extra money would help see me through college. That financial plan was doomed before I left New Orleans. My parents had not been able to save any money for my tuition, and I didn't have any either. My dad was getting a promotion, which, ironically, would lead to him not traveling to New York just as I moved there. But even with the promotion, they could not afford NYU tuition, but I listened to their plan. The plan was such a mess that a week before I moved to New York, I was still preparing to go to LSU. At the last minute, my mom said things were set to go. On top of all of the loans I took out through the government, we took out a private loan through a website called My Rich Uncle. Yes, I know it screams shady, but remember, I was desperate and my mom was even more desperate to make things work for me. The interest rate was insane, but I didn't even know what an interest rate was back then. The loan would nearly double by the time I was out of college. The loan allowed me to get the basics for my new life in another state. I had a lot of doubts about the situation from a monetary perspective, but I trusted that my parents had a solid plan. Off we all went on the train. They laugh now when telling me the story of how they stood on a corner of Union Square outside of my dorm crying before boarding the train back to New Orleans without me.

I was completely unprepared financially for college, but since I didn't understand much about money, I didn't realize how much of a stretch it was for me to even think about attending NYU. I often meet people who can't understand my decision to go to a school I couldn't afford. I explain that someone taught them what "afford" meant. I really had no idea. There were certainly more reasonable options, but there was no one to teach me how to sit down and calculate financial decisions and how they would impact me. Thankfully, there was assistance through FAFSA, the Free Application for Federal Student Aid. I was surprised how much the government gave me for college through loans and grants. My parents said they had a plan and would be able to pay everything off without me having to pitch in, and I believed them. I never could have imagined the burden that debt would be in my future.

My parents insisted that going to NYU was an amazing opportunity that I could not pass up. I loved living in New York. NYU does not have a traditional campus, so the experience is like living in the city. Classes are scattered around Lower Manhattan. I loved the sense of freedom, and I had never been into the traditional campus lifestyle. Tuition aside, it was a perfect match.

My amazing mom even picked up a job cooking for a local priest so that she'd have money to send me every week. It was still a struggle to get the basics. I remember trying to buy a box of Cheerios from a drugstore during my first week there. It was seven dollars. I knew then I wasn't going to make it.

Exploring Majors

Even though I was serious about school, at eighteen, I just wasn't ready to commit to one career path. It was bizarre to me that I was expected to make a decision on what I wanted to do with my life when I barely had any life experience. I had always wanted to be a veterinarian because I loved animals. By the time I reached college, I realized I didn't want to put them to sleep, so I had to come up with a new plan. I didn't know what else to do at the time, but I loved my anatomy and biology classes and I was interested in helping people. So I went to college on the pre-med track. I always knew I did not want to be a doctor.

Then I took a biological anthropology class and loved it, so I took a few more. I figured that would be my major, but then I realized that being interested in the classes was different from dedicating my life to work in the field. I was not enjoying my pre-med classes at all. The breaking point came two weeks into my calculus class, in the first semester of my sophomore year.

I was looking for inspiration to struggle through another night of calculus homework. When things are tough, I envision my future goal, remember how a rough spot fits into the larger picture, and get back at it. But since I didn't really want to be a doctor, there was nothing to pull motivation from.

I thought back to four-year-old Sheba having a picnic with my mom, and I knew that I wasn't willing to give my all to my pre-med classes. So I let go. It was time to quit this med school path. I went back to my dorm that evening and dropped all of my classes. I went to my roommates to find out what they were taking. They were completely freaked out by the fact that I had no classes. That was the first time quitting really affected my future in a positive way. Now, when I am hesitant to walk away from something because I fear I won't come up with a better plan, I think back to that moment and how less fulfilling my life would be if I had continued forcing myself to do something that I knew wasn't for me. I calmed my roommates down and asked them for their schedules for inspiration. One was taking a journalism class, but she said it was supposed to be hard. I had never even thought about taking a journalism class before, but after suffering through calculus, I figured it had to be better because it involved writing. I had always loved writing, and my English classes were my absolute favorite. I had always overlooked my love of words because I kept hearing that most English majors become teachers. At that point, however, it didn't matter. I just wanted to enjoy my education and not dread going to class every day. I would figure out a plan later. I signed up for a creative writing class too. I figured I would find my way by starting with classes I already knew I would enjoy.

Even then, I never ever thought about working in TV news. When I signed up for the journalism class, the idea of being a newspaper reporter crossed my mind, but I didn't even give that any serious thought. However, I should have been considering a career in broadcast television. There were many factors that made TV news a good fit for me. I loved writing. I was great at public speaking and loved to read. I am naturally curious and a great researcher. I love talking to people and having good conversations, and a great interview is really just an informative conversation. I took a sharp detour off the pre-med track and was put right on track to my future. But at the time, I thought I was just taking another random class.

The Introduction to Journalism class was tough, but I did enjoy it. It was a big class, held in an auditorium, but it was broken down into smaller classes that met on another day of the week. I loved my writing assignments, but my grades were disappointing at first. I talked with my instructor in the smaller class, asking him how I could improve, and he started giving me even more detailed feedback on my papers. The class would examine and critique media coverage. For the final paper, in which we had to include a firsthand account, I criticized the portrayal of juvenile delinquents in the media. While working on the assignment, I had taken a taxi and was chatting with my driver. I learned that my driver had a criminal record as a child. He agreed to let me interview him for my paper. I loved being able to tell someone's story and put it in a larger context with statistics and facts. By the end of the class, my grade had improved drastically.

In my sophomore year, I finally knew that I wanted to focus on writing. I was enjoying school a lot more, but I also had a growing sense of guilt over how much school was costing my parents. I had planned on being pre-med, so I figured I wouldn't have any problem making money in the future. But now that I was focusing on writing, I wondered what I would do if I got out of school and didn't land a high-paying job. The longer I stayed at NYU, the more I felt at home, but I also felt more pressure to be amazingly successful when I graduated. And honestly, I still had no idea what I would do with these writing classes in the future. I pushed forward anyway. I was in the liberal arts school but had my eye on NYU's Gallatin School of Individualized Study, where you could invent your own major. I wanted to study imagination and how it affected writing. I planned to combine journalism and creative writing classes. I was really excited about it, applied, and got accepted to the school. Just when I felt as if I was getting things together, everything started falling apart.

3

Getting through Rough Spots

.

*All endings are also beginnings. We just don't know it at
the time.*

Mitch Albom,
The Five People You Meet in Heaven

Being Derailed

In December 2008, I flew home for Christmas break. When it was time to
go back to school, my parents said they were waiting on some money to pay
my tuition. It wasn't odd for my parents to still be scrambling to catch up on
tuition two or three days before I headed to school, so I didn't think much of
it at first. But this time was different.

School started, and I still wasn't there. I found out that my parents had
been asking for extensions on my tuition payments and not making those
payments, so the debt was piling up. My tuition balance was $24,000, and
that was after applying all of the loans I had taken out. I knew that my parents
would never be able to come up with that money, and I wouldn't be going
back to NYU. It was too late to enroll in any other college, and before I could
even do that, NYU had to be paid the money it was owed before it would
release my transcript to another school.

I had worked hard and was on the dean's list at NYU. Having to leave
New York made me feel as if I had done something wrong. Even though I
had the grades, the test scores, scholarships, none of it was enough. I now
wonder how I could not have known how unrealistic the plan was to begin
with. Despite the obvious signs, it wasn't until that moment that I knew I had
made the wrong decision going there. I was just as smart and hardworking as
any other student at NYU, but I didn't have a rich family or financial stability
like many of my classmates. It was one of the hardest times I have ever been
through. School had always helped me rise above my reality, and without it,
I felt stagnant and helpless. How could I ever get past all of this and be better

if I wasn't even going to be able to finish college? While this secret frustration was inside of me, I told myself to get over it, and soon enough I did. NYU is just one school, I told myself. New York is not going anywhere.

I figured that for the rest of the semester, I would find a job in New Orleans, save some money, and go from there. But it wasn't that easy. No one wanted to hire me. No stores in the mall, no grocery stores—nowhere. I had no real job experience and no car. And so I ended up sitting in my house for nearly the entire semester. All of my friends had gone back to college, so I started writing a novel. I put myself on a schedule, waking up early to write and setting page goals. I still have that story saved somewhere on my computer, but I couldn't tell you what it was about anymore. I wrote nearly a hundred pages, but I was editing so much as I went along that the story wasn't flowing. That unfinished book is the most productive thing that came out of those months. Thankfully, one of my friends was at college nearby in Baton Rouge, which is about an hour from New Orleans. On many weekends, she would pick me up so I could spend time with her. Our little adventures helped keep me from going insane.

Getting Back on Track

When it was almost time for school to start again, my mom worked one of her miracles. My parents hadn't been able to pay NYU any money, and neither had I since I wasn't working. My mom talked to someone at the university who agreed to give me a copy of my transcript, even though I still owed NYU more than $20,000. I felt as if there were a higher power watching over me and helping me move forward.

By then, there were only a few more days before the University of New Orleans (UNO) kicked off classes for the fall semester of 2009, but I wasn't going to miss another semester. I talked with a counselor who helped me choose among the classes that were still available. I was interested in journalism, so she insisted that I enroll in a class called Inside the Newsroom. She said it was being taught by an amazing guest professor, but because students needed special permission to register, many hadn't bothered to take the extra step to sign up. The class would change my life. Just like that, I was back on track. I even found a part-time job working for a store that made paraphernalia for local fraternities and sororities. It felt great to lessen the financial burden for my family.

I wasn't excited about going to UNO. In my circle of friends, "UNO" stood for "University of No Opportunity," but I was so glad to be back in school that it didn't matter. It wouldn't take me long to realize how wrong I was and how much opportunity UNO would provide for me. I took extra hours to make up for the semester that I missed. So I was super busy with school, and I was working at the store. UNO is a commuter school. Most students live off campus, so there wasn't a big sense of campus life. I felt too busy to be involved with any organizations, so I kept to myself for the most part. I left the social side of college behind at NYU. I wasn't thinking about making new friends or going to college parties. I just wanted to make up for the time I missed and keep working toward my future.

And the future seemed very bright in the *Inside the Newsroom* class with guest professor Kim Bondy. Kim had just left CNN and moved back home to New Orleans. She was teaching only one class while she was finishing her MBA at UNO. I was lucky enough to be one of about a dozen students in her class. I absolutely adored and admired her from the start.

I was still trying to get everything together when school began. I had just started working, so I didn't have enough money to buy all of my books. After the first day of class, I told Kim I wouldn't be able to get the book until I got my next paycheck. She replied that she was new to teaching and maybe the class didn't need a book. I don't know if she even remembers that moment, but I thought it was remarkable, because she could have made me feel bad or given me a hard time. Instead, she blew it off as if it was no big deal and

Kim Bondy and Soledad O'Brien. (Photograph by author)

My mentor, Kim Bondy. (Photograph by author)

My mentor, Soledad O'Brien. (Photograph by author)

asked me more about myself. I had a lot of questions for her too. I had never met a woman I wanted to be like in a professional sense until I met her. She was intelligent without being pretentious, fabulous but laid-back, and one of the most genuine people I have ever met. No more flip-flopping, no more uncertainty about my career path—I wanted to be just like her.

Kim had worked in the news business in nearly every capacity: anchoring, producing, and creating new shows. She could answer students' endless questions about what it was really like to work in a newsroom. Each class, we had to pitch a story, just like reporters in newsrooms. We would all discuss the story that each student pitched, and she would give us feedback. Since she had so many connections in the industry, the class benefited from many guests, who video-chatted about what their jobs entailed and answered our questions. Our guests ranged from local documentary producers, to a field producer from CNN, to Hoda Kotb from *Today*.

Soledad O'Brien, Kim's best friend, visited our class. I was excited because I was familiar with her work, especially her *Black in America* series on CNN. She let us ask her anything we wanted, and when the class was over, Kim pulled me aside to introduce us. Kim told Soledad that I was her star student. As we were saying goodbye, Soledad quickly mentioned that I should come to New York to intern with her in the summer. I got excited about the idea, but then I blew it off. I was sure she had said it only to be nice.

Declaring My Major

That first semester at UNO, I was nearly a junior and needed to declare a major. I had decided to pursue journalism. The only problem was that UNO didn't have a journalism major and didn't offer many journalism classes. So I went with English. I had the option to concentrate on certain subjects. I chose journalism and creative writing. I still think about how much stress and confusion I could have saved myself by focusing on my love of writing at the beginning of college. English had always been my favorite subject in school, and I had really enjoyed my writing assignments. But I never even considered pursuing writing in college or beyond because I didn't think it would ensure a stable future. In the back of my mind, I still wondered if being an English major could prepare me for life after college. Majoring in English gave me an edge over other applicants when applying for the job at WWL, but we're not at that part of the story yet. When I declared my major, I thought I would work in print journalism, but I kept hearing that print news was a dying business. That didn't totally turn me off, but what really pushed me to broadcast news was Kim's class. I realized that broadcast journalism was based on good writing too. And I knew that I would be happy as long as I was writing. Kim insisted that if I learned what I needed to in my internships, my major wouldn't be that important.

As the summer got closer, I started planning to make up the semester I missed. I also had a lingering thought that I should email Soledad to find out more about the internship she had mentioned. I thought it would be silly not to follow up with her, so I did. I must admit I was surprised she even answered my email and was even more surprised when she said that I could intern at CNN with her for a few weeks. All I had to do was find a place to live in New York. I was working, so I was making some money. But it was nowhere near enough for any of the short-term rental options in New York. Eventually, I emailed Soledad and asked if she had any suggestions about affordable temporary housing. She wrote back that I could use her apartment, since her family was living in their summer home. I'd had my doubts about Soledad's offer from day one, but that email officially made it all too good to be true. She laughs now when I tell her that, at that point, I knew there was a slight chance I'd be kidnapped on arrival, but even that couldn't keep me from the amazing opportunity.

That's how I landed my first internship and found my way back to New York. Just a few months before, I was broke, jobless, out of school, and feeling completely hopeless, but that opportunity turned everything around. After that, I told myself I would never doubt my future again just because there were no immediate solutions in front of me. I learned to have faith in the bad times too, because that's when I would need it the most.

4

Interning at CNN

Learn everything you can, anytime you can, from anyone you can—there will always come a time when you will be grateful you did.

Sarah Caldwell

I get lots of emails from students who are interested in journalism and stressing out over their choice of college and major. Let me tell you: It's really not worth the stress. Successful people come from many different colleges, and some did not go to college at all. And these successful people majored in subjects all across the board. Plus, if you want to work in TV, internships are way more important than where you go to school or what your major is. I didn't graduate from a prestigious school or great journalism program, so how did I soar to the top of the game over people with better resources? It was my internships. They helped level the playing field. It didn't matter what school I went to or what I already knew. Interning put me in the workplace I wanted to land a job in and gave me access to everything I needed to prepare myself.

There are many components to working in a newsroom that I would never have gotten from class. I was dreaming of working in the news, but there is so much to the industry that I never even considered because those parts didn't become a reality until I was doing them. Now that I have been working in news for a few years, there are many factors that I tell aspiring journalists to consider before pursuing a job in the industry.

Things to Consider before Entering the News Industry

Being on TV Isn't as Glamorous as It Looks

Look, I get it. The TV cameras, bright lights, outfits, hair and makeup—our jobs look glamorous. But trust me. TV news is not about glamour, especially at the local level. I do my own hair and makeup, and buy all of the clothing I wear on TV. This is typical unless you work in a really big market. Many times when I am in the field, I am scrambling to get my work done in New Orleans heat, which sometimes makes me feel like I am actually frying, and barely have time to fix my hair or reapply makeup between live shots.

I have done live shots soaking wet many times and for many reasons: storm coverage, regular rainstorms, unexpected street flooding, or a water-main break. Storm coverage is a blessing in disguise appearance-wise, because people's expectations drop. My hair is all over my head, but viewers think, "OK, we see her getting rained on. We get it."

In worse scenarios, the rain comes during a story that has nothing to do with the rain. I was standing outside of a bar once, doing live shots on a robbery, when the skies opened up. There was so much wind and rain that the producer told me to just wrap up the live shot because no one could understand what I was saying anyway. As the morning went on, the weather cleared up, but by then, my hair was a frizzy mess and my makeup was all over my face. I'm sure viewers who were waking up toward the end of the show were thinking, "Why does she look like that?"

There Is a Lot of Writing Involved

Reporters write their own stories for live shots and for pieces on the evening news. They don't just say what comes off the top of their heads, unless it's breaking news. Even then, they usually have a few notes to make sure they don't ramble. Producers write everything that anchors say, but anchors make changes so that things are written in their own style. Traffic reporters and meteorologists do not write scripts. They ad-lib. My first paid job in a newsroom was as an associate producer, and all I did was write scripts every day, for hours. Now, I write my own scripts for my show, *The 504.*

We Work All Day

The news is on every single day, which means that someone is working every day, at all points of the day, to make that happen. The lights never go off in a newsroom. We work through holidays and hurricanes, and everything in between. Everyone has a set schedule, and that may include working overnight. My first work shift in the newsroom was from one thirty in the morning to seven in the morning. Shifts may include weekends or late nights. Even though I am typically off on weekends, I could be called to fill in for someone, to cover breaking news, or to be part of election coverage.

During hurricanes, when everyone is evacuating, we go into twenty-four-hour mode at the station. Everyone at the station from reporters to anchors to photographers "moves" to the station, sleeping there when they are not actively taking a shift working.

February, May, November, and, technically, July are called sweeps rating periods, during which the number of viewers matters the most. Nielsen Media Research collects information on what channels people watch and exactly who in the household watches the channel. No one at the station is allowed to take vacation in February, May, or November. The no-vacation policy is not enforced during July at my station.

Being on TV Doesn't Necessarily Mean You Make a Lot of Money

TV internships may be unpaid, and entry-level jobs in the newsroom are not lucrative at all. My first job as an associate producer paid ten dollars an hour, and I worked part time. The first reporting job I was offered, in Lafayette, Louisiana, paid $24,000 a year. In small markets, the people on-air usually pay for their own hair, makeup, and wardrobe expenses that come out of the small salary they earn. People think that everyone on TV has a lot of money, when, actually, many low-profile jobs outside of the news industry offer more rewarding salaries. The good news is that the further you climb, the more opportunities there are to earn more money. To make more money, you may have to move, or you could work two jobs to have a decent income until a better position becomes available. The last option was my tactic for surviving my first job in news.

Newsrooms Have to Work around Deadlines and Staffing Limitations

Viewers are quick to criticize the content of news shows. People demand that every event in their area be covered. They question why a story is covered in a certain way or why more attention was not given to a certain victim or crime. I used to be one of those people watching the news and picking it apart through the screen. I must admit that I went into the newsroom with a bit of a superhero attitude. I wanted to fix everything people criticize about the news. But once I was in the door, I realized that a news organization is a company like any other workplace. At the end of the day, companies have money to hire only a certain number of people. In a newsroom, every day, there is more news to cover than reporters to cover it and photographers to shoot it.

Sometimes, when a story isn't being covered, it's because there simply wasn't someone to cover it. Sometimes, a reporter calls in sick, so there are only two reporters left covering everything that happened between ten o'clock in the morning and six in the evening. I do get frustrated when I want to do a story that I think is important but can't because of a lack of resources. For instance, the photographers on staff may already be working with other reporters on more pressing stories.

Once I was in the business, I also realized that what a reporter covers in a day is often not their choice. Reporters attend meetings with newsroom managers and producers every morning and evening to decide what will be covered and how it will be covered. In our newsroom, the morning show crew kind of functions as a separate entity, mainly due to our crazy hours, so we have our own informal meetings. Sometimes, we get to cover the story we want to, but many times, we have to cover what our managers have decided needs to be covered for the day. Even if we do get to cover the story we want, there are deadlines and time constraints that often keep reporters from putting a story together exactly as they want to. The news comes on at the same time every day, so there is no such thing as saying, "This story could be better, so I will just keep working on it." Something has to be on the TV screen.

The Business Is Changing

With news available on the internet and social media, fewer people get their news from a newscast. When the evening news airs, people already know the big news stories of the day. Fewer people watching the news means lower ratings, which means less revenue. News stations are looking for ways to cut costs. One cost-cutting tactic is to hire more MMJs, or multimedia journalists, who can shoot and edit their own pieces. That way, a station can hire fewer photographers. Many future jobs will require reporters to shoot and edit their own work.

School Is Not as Important as Experience and Connections

One of the common misconceptions about journalism is that it requires a certain amount of formal schooling or knowledge from having studied a certain major. As I mentioned, people who work in newsrooms come from different educational backgrounds. Some went to very prestigious undergraduate schools, and some went on to graduate school. Newsroom staff at WWL have majored in various areas. I went with English, but there are mass communications majors, biology majors, political science majors, and, of course, communications and broadcast majors. One can become a journalist having majored in anything, but it was helpful for me to learn skills such as broadcast writing (which is a specific writing style) and editing. A better school or a certain major doesn't guarantee that someone does well in this field.

Understand Markets

A chef at a local chain restaurant and one at the most popular restaurant in the country have very different lives, jobs, and salaries, even though they are both chefs. The same applies to those working in the news industry. News markets or regions are ranked based on the size of the audience. Nielsen Media Research ranks 210 markets. The rankings of local markets can be found with a simple internet search. Typically, the higher the market—and the more viewers—the more money a station makes, and therefore, the more money the staff makes. As of 2017, New Orleans was market fifty-one, and New York was number one. In New York, there's a bigger chance that news anchors will make more money and benefit from sweet perks, such as hair and makeup, than there is in smaller markets. The low-viewer markets are known as starter markets in the news world. They tend to hire people straight out of college. Sometimes, one person will handle anchoring, producing, and reporting in a newscast. Journalists typically don't stay in those markets a long time. They get experience and then move to a higher market with better pay. I wasn't thinking about any of that as I fought to make my way into the business, but as I started interning, I learned a lot of things about the business that I never could have understood without being in the newsroom.

Arriving in New York

My first internship was at CNN during the summer before my senior year of college. Even as I packed my bags for the trip to New York, I couldn't understand why Soledad wanted to help me. She didn't know anything about me. Why was she letting me live in her place (which, by the way, was amazing)?

The elevator opened into the apartment, as it was the only unit on the entire floor. It was huge, with a great view of the Chelsea neighborhood in Manhattan. The buildings reminded me of those I would pass as I was walking to my classes at NYU and wonder who lived there. Soledad and her husband, or one of their guests, dropped by occasionally. But mostly, it was just me in this giant apartment. My friends from NYU were still in the city, so I already had good friends to hang out with. I didn't arrive with much money—maybe a hundred dollars—but my parents promised to send what they could to help. I knew how to get by on PB&J sandwiches and cereal and milk. I had everything I needed to make the most of those five weeks. I even decided to take the subway by myself. Yes, I had lived in New York for nearly two years before, but I always avoided the subway unless I was with a friend. I couldn't forget the image of people stuck underground after the 9/11 terrorist attacks. I was determined, however, to venture out of my comfort zone in every way imaginable.

Putting Myself out There

The CNN New York bureau is in the Time Warner Center, and when I walked in I was definitely out of my comfort zone. At the time, Soledad was a special correspondent and anchor with the *In America* division. The unit covered underreported stories and underrepresented communities. I was not an official intern. Soledad, a get-it-done-no-matter-what kind of person, was determined to have me intern with her, so she made it work. I never filled out an application. When I arrived, I just signed in as Soledad's guest for the day—every day for several weeks. The first day, I felt uncomfortable as I walked into the office. I had imagined seeing stiff CNN robots who only worked. No laughing, no joking, no mistakes—just work. A million doubts ran through my mind. Would I be able to do the work here? What if people don't want to help me?

My experience was the complete opposite. Everyone went out of their way to make me feel welcome. Get this: Soledad's assistant asked if I wanted coffee, instead of sending me out for his. CNN was a huge place with lots of people running around. I had to walk through them every day to get to the *In America* unit, which was nestled in its own little corner. Since the division was tucked away, I felt sheltered, even in such a big place.

Soledad's assistant suggested I work in Soledad's office, since she wasn't there often. She had an amazing view overlooking Central Park. I spent my first few days thinking, "This is pretty sweet." Then, I remembered that I was there to get to know people, to make connections, to learn things, and to be uncomfortable. After a few days, I told Soledad's assistant that I wanted to work in the big room where everyone else was. I instantly started meeting more people and was asked to help with more assignments.

Learning from Every Assignment

On most days, I worked from ten in the morning until six at night. My internship at CNN would be the last time I worked in a news environment and had a normal schedule. Even after I realized that everyone was nice and helpful, I was still intimidated by the work—because it was *CNN*, a national news outlet. In my mind, "national" meant that the work would be harder, the people would be more serious, and the expectations would be higher. I was ready to work hard and learn from every moment. In the next few sections, I break down my different assignments, how I tackled them, and how I took something away from each that I could use to grow. As I was learning, I was writing down as much as I could, so that I would have something to refer back to if I got stuck on a task. Taking notes is such a simple thing that I almost forgot to mention it. Time is precious, and one of the simple ways I respect someone's time is by taking notes when they are teaching me something. Now that I am on the other side of the intern-staff relationship, there is nothing more annoying than having an intern ask for help with something they've already been taught. Take notes. That is all. Let's carry on.

Transcribing Speeches

Soledad gives speeches all over the country: at conferences, graduations, and award ceremonies. My first assignment didn't seem so bad. I was asked to make transcripts of those speeches from the original copies, which were scribbled on random sheets of paper. In any other setting, I probably would have blown this off as busywork, but because I was so happy to be there, I decided to make the most out of every little thing. Instead of mindlessly typing, I started paying attention to what Soledad had written. Her speeches contained a lot of great advice. She wrote about being challenged about her race, because she comes from a black-Cuban-Irish background. She eventually stood up for herself and refused to cower when people said she wasn't black enough or wasn't a Latina. She also discussed how terrible she thought she was when she first started reporting. She made a list of all the things she wanted to improve on and then worked on them one by one. Great! If Soledad didn't start out perfectly, I didn't have to either.

Logging Tape

Hands down, the most annoying and tedious thing about creating a news story is logging, which involves making transcripts from video footage. You have to type out conversations from recorded interviews and mark the time that specific phrases are said. Then, you use those time codes when you write the story, so if you want to use that part of the conversation, you'll know exactly where to find it. I logged footage from "Black in America: Churched," Soledad's third documentary in the *Black in America* series, which explores issues and events in the black community.

My most time-consuming logging project, however, was a ninety-minute police training video that turned into a twenty-page transcript. Although it was tedious, logging allowed me to see how journalists cut down hours of video footage to a few minutes for a news story or documentary.

Lots of Researching

Then there was research, research, and more research. During my first week, Soledad was scheduled to interview a law professor at Harvard University about his new book. To help prepare, I looked up book reviews and drafted interview questions, and then Soledad took me with her to the event. She introduced me to everyone, not as her intern, but as one of her coworkers. I never mentioned it to her, but that made me feel special. I looked up to her, and she thought of me as her equal. In the interview, she even asked some of the questions I had written for her. I took note of which ones she skipped and which ones she tweaked so that I could come up with even better questions next time.

I did a lot of research to help Soledad prepare for panels and interviews. My focus was always to make sure I had the facts right. It didn't matter how insightful I thought my questions were or how much research I did, if the information was not correct, all of that work was a waste of time. And the more work I did, the less intimidated I was. I could do research. In fact, I loved doing research for school papers. Honestly, this was no different.

Finding Interviews

Of course, every task wasn't that easy. For one assignment, a senior producer asked me to call Arizona law offices to find an immigrant who was struggling to return home to Central America. She wanted to do a story on someone who had come to America but was not able to stay because of the economy. I tried hard not to give her a deer-in-the-headlights look and said, "OK, sure!" I had no idea where to start. I had never had an assignment like that. I felt intimidated and overwhelmed again, but I pushed those feelings aside and got to work. I looked up a list of pro bono lawyers in Arizona— thinking they would be more likely to deal with immigrants who were struggling financially—and started making calls. I was shocked to hear a 911 operator on the other end of the line. I had dialed 9-1-1 to dial out of the office instead of 9-1. Even after I stopped calling the police, I didn't have much success. I called about seventy-five law offices—yes, seventy-five. By four o'clock in the afternoon, hours had gone by, and I still had no leads.

Finally, after hours of searching the internet, I lucked up on an article about how the Guatemalan consulate in Los Angeles had been buying two bus tickets a week to send immigrants back home. I began calling consulates in Arizona and finally felt as if I was making headway. Then, I found an article about a group in New York that was helping Ecuadorans return home and another group in Queens running a similar program. I reached out to them, but the person who answered the phone spoke only Spanish. I gave the organization's contact information to the senior producer since she spoke Spanish and told her that I thought they might be helpful to the story. Sure enough, after a phone call, she told me that the group was perfect, even though they were not in Arizona.

The next week, interviews were set up with the Guatemalan consulate, the Ecuadoran group in New York, and an immigrant returning to Central America. As a reward for my hard work, I was allowed to attend the shoot. I traveled with Soledad and her crew to Brooklyn for an interview with a man from Ecuador who had a tragic story of trying to return to his country. The next stop was Queens, where Soledad interviewed the spokesman for the group helping immigrants return to Ecuador.

The final piece was a minute- or two-minute-long CNN story titled "Escaping America," which included the two interviews that I helped set up and a story on the Guatemalan consulate. I no longer felt like a visitor at CNN, watching what everyone did around me. I had become a part of the team.

Little Assignments Lead to Bigger Ones

That senior producer's name was Rose Arce. She gave me a chance and challenged me. She made my time at CNN a true learning experience. The immigrant story assignment helped me win her over. My reward: more work! The next task involved helping with a story on a controversial Senate bill that would require officers to ask the legal status of anyone they arrest. Opponents claimed it legalized racial profiling. I needed to find a copy of the police training video that was being used in Arizona. After logging the ninety-minute video, I had to arrange an interview with the police chief in Mesa, Arizona. After several days of phone calls, I secured the interview. The scheduling didn't work for the person who was supposed to do the interview on camera, so the senior producer told me to do a phone interview and write a story with the information I gathered. Good thing I had paid attention to what the story was about.

Even by my last week, however, I still had not worked with the executive producer of the department. She seemed friendly, and someone suggested that I get to know her. I went to her office and asked her more about her role. She took the time to ask me more about myself and gave me some quick career tips. The next day, when she needed something done, she came to me. My assignment was to put together bios for a nationwide list of pastors from different churches and denominations being considered for a panel. It sounded easy enough, but the assignment took me an entire evening and night, and went into the next morning. Some of the pastors were obscure and hard to find online (I wasn't allowed to make calls for this assignment).

After I turned in the list of pastors, the executive producer said that I had done such a great job that she wanted me to work on something else for her. I spent the last two days of the internship looking up each pastor's stance on particular issues (including gay rights, the role of women in the church, and HIV/AIDS). The hard part was that I couldn't just do a simple internet search and click on each pastor's name to find the information. No one would have randomly compiled what I was looking for into one perfect article. So I had to search through the internet for old articles and videos of each pastor and hope that they mentioned something about one of these issues and talked about it enough that I could understand their particular view.

I wish someone had told me before I started that some information is impossible to find, and I would just have to accept that. There were times when I spent hours looking for information and felt as if I was doing something wrong because I couldn't find it. For instance, when I was asked to find the racial makeup of Arizona's police force or statistics on the black gay community, I couldn't find much. When I finally checked in with the producer, she said, "I know—impossible, right?" Some research quite simply doesn't exist or isn't accessible to the public, and realizing that helped me to stop doubting my abilities. I started to trust that if I couldn't find the information, there was probably a good reason.

Today, if I were in that position I would say, "Hey, I've been looking for this for x amount of time, and I'm not finding anything. This is where I've looked. Is there anywhere else you think I should try? Is there anything else you want me to look for?" In some cases, I found something of related interest through my research. When that happened, I would pass the information along. For instance, while I didn't find an immigrant in Arizona who matched the description from the producer, I had found groups in New York and Los Angeles where such people might be contacted. I told the producer that I hadn't found exactly what she wanted but that I had found something else that might work. And sure enough, it did.

I left New York feeling back on track to a successful future. I was uncomfortable my first few days at CNN, but by the end of those five weeks, I was more confident in myself and my ability to be successful in the industry. The most comforting knowledge was that even on the national level of the news business, there was no magic happening. The work was all phone calls, research, and brainstorming. It was work that anyone could do. The experience reignited my excitement about the future. I had my senior year of college ahead of me, but all I could think about was getting back to working in the news. It was one thing to sit in a classroom and talk about doing research, developing story ideas, and interviewing, but the classroom experience was nothing like diving in and learning firsthand what worked and what didn't.

Being Dragged across the Finish Line

Officially an English major, I started my senior year feeling hopeful, and eager to get through college and out into the real world. This was the end of the road. The hardest parts were over—or so I thought. I had a rude awakening regarding a recurring theme: I was short on tuition again. Not long after I started going back to school in New Orleans, I had started working a part-time retail job. I didn't make a lot of money, but I was able to buy my school books and pitch in with small things for the house, since I was back living at home with my parents. I didn't have any money to put aside, so I had no savings. I could not pay my tuition. My parents pleaded with the bursar's office at UNO to make a payment plan for me, but the office wasn't bending. Kim happened to be on campus that day and ran into my parents. She told them she would see what she could do. Before I knew it, Soledad emailed to ask exactly what my balance was. It was close to $3,000. She wrote the check as if it were nothing. Soledad had been helping young girls across the country pay for school for years. During my financial trouble, she was finally starting an official foundation to put young girls through college.

It started off as the Starfish Foundation. Soledad loves to tell the story of the man walking along the beach picking up starfish and chucking them back into the water, because the tide was down and they were stuck on land. In the story, someone walks up to him and tells him that there are too many starfish to make a difference. The guy picks up a starfish and throws it in, saying, "It made a difference to that one."

Soledad was definitely making a difference in my life, and I couldn't thank Kim enough for pulling Soledad in to rescue me. Soledad's organization is now known as the PowHERful Foundation, because of its focus on empowering young women. Without the foundation, I could have been a college dropout. I started thinking that I must really be meant to do something great, because someone out there was knocking brick walls down so that I could keep moving forward. So forward I went into my senior year.

Timing

My senior year flew by. Kim suggested that I get an internship during my final semester. because it would make for good timing. If a station wanted to hire me, I would be nearly out of school and able to accept the job. These days, I hear from a lot of high-school students who want to be in the news business and want to start doing internships now, but they run into roadblocks because of their age. Some newsrooms have laws regarding the age of employees, including interns. Other stations require that interns be in college or receiving some type of college credit. Stations tend to prefer juniors and seniors because they are closer to entering the workforce and are less likely to change their career paths.

I always tell these high-school students not to stress out over not being able to intern. I didn't complete my first internship until the summer before my senior year in college, and I don't feel as if I missed out on anything. High-school students interested in the news business should find someone they admire on local TV and send that person an email asking about their vocations. I get emails like this from young students all the time, and I am always eager to answer. I also suggest asking the person if it's possible to shadow them for a day, to get a sense of what a newsroom is like and to start building relationships with people in the industry.

Many who have dreamed of being a news anchor don't want to hear this, but it's impossible to decide on a career path without spending time in that particular work environment. Saying that I wanted to be a neonatologist was a lot more appealing to me than the idea of going through medical school or being around sick babies all day. It's easy to be fascinated with the idea of being a TV news anchor, but it's a very different world behind the scenes. The job requires a day-to-day lifestyle that one can't get a sense of through the TV screen. The great thing is that, nowadays, it's simple to learn on your own. To practice, many people get a camera, shoot video, install editing software on their computers, make their own stories, and even post them online. Nothing is stopping anyone from doing journalistic work completely on their own.

I have the same advice for people who want to enter the business later in life, but who don't have access to a newsroom to learn the skills they need. You can buy the equipment or find a friend who has it, and go for it. Once you are happy with the quality of your work, you can send it to a newsroom and apply for jobs.

When it comes to experience, it's all about quality not quantity. If you can't get an internship until the senior year of college, it really is fine. I know that we are a society of overachievers, but don't stress for no reason. Some of my classmates thought they knew what they wanted to do and started interning when we were college freshmen, but some of them did not even decide to go into the fields they were interning in. I didn't start working on career development until my last year of college. I think it's important to enjoy life at all times and not put so much emphasis on crafting a perfect future, especially to the point that the present is filled with anxiety. I also don't believe in doing something just because it looks good on paper. Life is too short—and there are lots of opportunities that look good on paper and are also enjoyable.

5

Interning at a Local News Station

Tell me and I forget; teach me and I may remember;
involve me and I learn.

Chinese proverb

Landing an Internship

I didn't know how to get an internship at a local station, and I couldn't find any information online. I found phone numbers for each station and called. I knew there were other opportunities available in radio and print, but I limited my search to TV stations. The goal was to work in TV, so I wanted to be around people who worked in TV. I had my eye on WWL, since I watched the morning show while getting dressed for school, but I never got a response to any of my emails or phone calls. I called WDSU, another local station, and was told I needed to speak with the executive producer, who just happened to be finishing up the list of intern candidates for the semester. She added my name to the list. There were no questions and no interview. Just like that, I secured my next internship.

The internship was easy to land, and I already had some skills from interning at CNN. But none of that was any help for my nerves. I was just as anxious heading into WDSU as I was heading into CNN. Once again, I had no idea what to expect. The executive producer I had spoken with on the phone turned out to be the internship supervisor. On the first day, she gave her new dozen interns a tour of the newsroom and a current events quiz. I had certainly read the news, but I don't remember any of us doing exceptionally well. I made a mental note to start consuming even more news. She gave us work sheets to fill out that would require us to meet everyone who worked at the station. We were also given a packet that outlined our responsibilities as interns. Here was the shocker: She would give us college credit whether we showed up or not. "It's a trap," I thought to myself. She's trying to trick us. No one would possibly consider not showing up for their internship and just taking the credit. Turns out, only two or three of us were showing up after the first few weeks. And it wasn't a trap. It was a way to weed out people who didn't really want to be there.

Typical Internship Duties

Our assignments were simple—as in, elementary. Answer the phones. Make copies. Deliver scripts to the anchors. All of the stories that anchors read in the teleprompter are printed out, with each story on its own sheet of paper. That way, if the teleprompter is not working properly, an anchor can easily keep up with stories in the newscast. Technology is advancing so quickly that paper scripts are being phased out and replaced with iPads. Interns also had to make beat calls, which were calls to local police and fire departments to see if they were responding to any new situations that might make a good story. There was a list of about twenty different numbers, and we were required to call them every hour. Ninety-nine percent of the time, the person who answered the phone said that absolutely nothing was happening.

Answering the phones was a nightmare. People would call the station because they were angry about something an anchor said, because a reporter mispronounced a word, because they wanted to know what time a soap opera aired, because they were mad at President Obama, because an anchor had on a sleeveless dress and "looked like a stripper" (yes, these were real calls). Just when you would think you'd heard it all, the phone would ring again. I didn't know how to get off the phone with those crazy people. I would get stuck on the phone for ten to fifteen minutes listening to someone rant, complain, or ask Harry Potter's age (yes, that also really happened).

Many of the calls were a waste of time, but I didn't want to act unprofessionally. Every now and then, someone would call with a legitimate news tip or great story idea. One day, a man called to say that a fire hydrant had been left on across the street from his business and the building was flooding. The man claimed that there was a ton of water, and he wanted us to come out and put it on the news. I thought it sounded like a good story, so I told one of the assignment editors who worked on the desk. He suggested I ask the man to send pictures. He did, and there could not have been more than an inch of water on the ground. I learned a good life and news lesson: Don't believe it until you see it for yourself or hear it from a reputable source.

Most of the interns spent the first few days awkwardly sitting around in the newsroom, making beat calls. I took a good look at that internship packet. If I did everything in the packet, in a few months, I was set to be a phone expert. I was going to have to make my own internship goals if I wanted to learn something useful. I branched out, talking with the reporters, producers, and photographers about what they did. Just like at CNN, almost everyone was eager to help. There was a lot I wanted to learn, and I was sitting in a room full of people who could help me learn it all. I had to dive in.

Exploring All Positions

My professor Kim Bondy had been a producer, so I thought I wanted to be a producer. I started spending my time with more producers, only to find that most producers in local newsrooms sit at their desks all day looking for content for the shows they produce. They write the stories that go in those shows, and then they go into the control room while the show happens. They make sure the reporter talks for the right amount of time. They communicate with the anchors about any changes during the show. And they time the show to make sure it begins and ends when it should. To be fair, there are field producers in larger markets who, as their name suggests, go out with the reporters to work on stories. That position does not exist in New Orleans.

I also was curious about reporting. One evening, my supervisor suggested that I go out with a reporter on a story. I introduced myself to a reporter named Gina Swanson and asked if I could tag along on her story shoot. I will never forget the first thing she said when we got in the car.

"I don't like interns."

I had chosen the wrong person. But I was stuck in the car, so I asked her a million questions anyway. She started to warm up once she realized I was familiar with the story she was working on for the day.

On my next shift, Gina was there, and I walked over to her desk. She was trying to catch up with a corrupt pastor and planned to ask him some questions while he was going into church Sunday morning. I was intrigued, so I asked to tag along. We met bright and early that Sunday morning, and from that day on, Gina referred to me as "her" intern. She explained that she did not like interns who did not want to work hard, and once she realized that I was serious, she loved having me by her side. I watched her bring stories to life through her interviews and live shots. After going out with her a few times, I knew for certain that I wanted to be a reporter.

I spent time with photographers and editors, even though I never considered working in those positions. I wanted to know all the parts that make things come together. I wrote scripts nearly every time I worked, and one of my reporter friends or the morning producer would edit them. I sat in the control room during the newscast to see the production aspect of the show. I visited the news set and watched the anchors do live shows. An associate producer taught me how to run teleprompter. I could find and cue tapes with old videos and interviews. I could write a competition log, which involved writing down what the other stations were covering for a newscast and in which order they aired the stories. I learned to write for the web and upload videos. No one cared that I had ditched the beat calls, and I never looked back. There were so many more productive tasks to do.

Scheduling Strategically

I had a full load of classes while I was interning. Though some internships have set schedules, which I think is more common, this one did not. My supervisor was very lax, so for the most part, we could work when we wanted. There were three typical shifts for anchors and reporters: morning (4:00 a.m. to noon), dayside (9:00 a.m. to 6:00 p.m.), and nightside (2:00 p.m. to 10:00 p.m.). Producers might have different schedules. For instance, morning show anchors come in around four in the morning, but some morning show producers come in around ten o'clock the previous night.

At WDSU, Rosa Flores was the peppy reporter for the morning show. After we talked, she suggested I shadow her in the mornings. Four o'clock in the morning seemed insanely early, but with that schedule, I would be able to spend some time at the station, go to class, and then have my evenings to do homework.

Twice a week, I arrived at the station at four in the morning, and it's true that the early bird gets the worm. The morning shift provided lots of opportunities to practice being a reporter, because the live shots were typically in one location throughout the morning show and there was a lot of downtime between Rosa's reports. Sometimes, Rosa used the downtime to work on her next live report. The time between reports could be a half hour, which can go by quickly if you are gathering information for breaking news, interviewing, and sending the producers cues for your report so that the video they play at the station matches what you are saying. But if it was a slow day with no breaking news, Rosa usually had a few minutes to spare before she went back on air. She would help me practice live shots and give me feedback. I would save the shots and show them to other reporters and producers.

When I heard how slow things were at the station on the weekends, I introduced myself to a weekend reporter named Tiffaney Bradley and started working with her on Saturday mornings. Also, the chief photographer took time on the weekends to teach me how to edit. I loved working with Gina, but she was on the dayside shift. During that time, photographers and reporters had less downtime between live shots, and there wasn't much free time for me to practice being in front of the camera. In morning and afternoon meetings, everyone on a shift gathers to decide what to cover for the day. Things can change a lot on the dayside shift. Let's say a reporter is told to follow up with the victim of a previous day's shooting. But right before the newscast at five o'clock in the evening, another shooting happens, and the one from yesterday is no longer a story. The reporters on the day shift don't do anywhere near the amount of live shots as the morning reporters. They may be live for the five o'clock or six o'clock evening shows, but they may also just create a story to contribute to the show and not go live at all, which would cut down on my opportunities to work on live shots. Since I had class early, the nightside shift wasn't an option.

Morning show reporters can have very long days. The morning show reporter I was shadowing was always at work for twelve or more hours every day. She would do her live shots in the morning and then come back and work on other stories. Some days, she was clearly tired and talked about making a goal of leaving the newsroom earlier. That never happened. I should say that her hard work eventually paid off. Rosa is now a correspondent for CNN. Reporters' lives vary drastically, depending on their schedules. However, no shift is better than another. It just depends on the reporter's preference. People who have worked on morning shows for years can't understand how the nightside people do it, and vice versa. I shadowed the morning show reporter only because it worked better for my school schedule. I never could have imagined that two years later I would have her exact shift and position at a competing station in the same market.

Building My Skill Set

I wasn't making any money interning, and I had quit my part-time job to focus on building my future career. I needed new skills for my resume so that I could eventually land a paid gig in the news. I was paying close attention to the actions of people in the newsroom and noted what skills they needed to get their jobs done. I would watch a reporter put a package together and think, "If I want to be a reporter, I should learn to put a package together too." (A "package" is a story made up of pieces of interviews, video, and, usually, a reporter's stand-up, which is the part where the reporter appears on camera during a story. Stand-ups are different from live shots, because the reporter tapes the piece and is not live when it airs on TV. These are the stories that are edited together for the news and complement what the anchors read from the desk.)

Here are some of the tasks on my skill-building list:

Broadcast Writing

Gina stressed the importance of writing for broadcast. She would make me write stories, and she wasn't shy about giving me critical feedback. She would also time me to make sure I could write them in under five minutes, which was still cutting me a lot of slack. Reporters and producers write a lot and write quickly, so I knew I would have to be a good writer no matter the route I chose.

I loved writing flowery sentences with multiple clauses and descriptive language. For TV news, all of that had to go. Broadcasting writing is simple and easy to listen to and digest. I had to remember that people are probably dressing their kids for school and trying to get ready for work as they listen to the news. They hear it one time and, in many cases, while they are doing something else, so the simpler the better. Viewers also have varying education levels. News writing is not the place to impress people with fancy language or lengthy descriptions. I had to get to the point. This lesson was difficult for me, but once I got the hang of it, the news writing style became second nature.

I would take stories from the Associated Press wire service or the newspaper that were meant to be read and rewrite them in a simpler format. The key was to start with an attention-grabbing sentence or phrase, but nothing too over the top, and then tell the story in under thirty seconds (in most cases). Explaining a complicated situation or story in such a short amount of time was also a huge challenge. And when done for an actual broadcast, the script has to match whatever video is available to go along with the story.

Editing and Shooting

During college, I would hear that the news business was changing. And now, I see it is. It's harder to find a reporting job in a lower market that won't require reporters to shoot and edit their own material. News stations are moving away from hiring photographers, editors, and reporters. They can cut costs by hiring one person to do all three. I also needed to be able to edit so that I could put together a tape of my work to find a job. I took an editing class through UNO's film program, which taught me the basics, and I worked on this skill at the station. Even though I was an English major, I took classes in other departments that I thought could help me down the line. I was never good at editing, but I knew the basics.

My resume had looked similar to many other aspiring reporters who just graduated from college: I had very little experience in the business, and I had done some internships. Several people told me that if I could shoot or edit, those skills might give me an edge over other candidates. I wanted to learn to shoot too, but I was told that because of union rules at the station, which are meant to protect employees, I wasn't allowed to shoot.

Interviewing

My first week at WDSU, my supervisor sent me and the new chief photographer to get some man on the street (MOS) interviews—that is, reactions from everyday people on the street. When all the reporters are out working on stories, producers can send interns out to do interviews. I was supposed to get at least three good sound bites about Edwin Edwards being released from prison. Edwards, a former Louisiana governor, had been sent to federal prison for corruption. I was excited to be out interviewing and thought that my assignment could not have been any easier. Half of the people I spoke to did not want to be on camera. Some had no idea what I was talking about, and others' answers were incoherent. Eventually, I managed to find three people who could speak intelligently on the subject and had strong opinions. Pieces of the interviews aired on the news, and the segment totaled approximately thirty seconds. I couldn't believe how much time and effort went into such a small part of the show.

I got lots more opportunities to do interviews. One day, I was sent to interview a pastor about a family conference at his church. The only information I had was that the conference would take place, and it was my job to find out more. I interviewed the pastor and members of the church who would be attending the conference. The interviews aired on television, and even though I was not in the shots, I was proud to know it was my hand behind the camera, holding the microphone.

When I did interviews during my internship at WDSU, I felt as if I didn't know enough. I was afraid I wouldn't ask good questions. Over the years, my interviewing skills have gotten much better with some very simple realizations. The more prepared I was for an interview, the less nervous I became. In those situations, I was confident that I knew what I was talking about and would ask relevant questions. One of the biggest mistakes I made early on was not listening to the responses of the person I was interviewing. I would ask a question and then focus on being ready to ask the next question. Soledad taught me that was a terrible habit. What if the person revealed that they were going to quit their job in the interview, and I missed it because I wasn't even listening? Even outside of the news business, I am a terrible listener. I retain information much better when it is visual, but I have trained myself to be a better listener.

Eventually, I stopped writing a list of questions to prepare for interviews and just made notes. The notes gave me a few cues to stay on track during the conversation. Having notes instead of questions also helped me feel as if I was having a conversation, while still revealing relevant information.

When I first started interviewing, I thought the more complicated the question, the smarter I would sound. I realized shorter and simpler questions were better and that sometimes the best way to keep the conversation going is with a simple "why" or "how." The best interviews I did felt like informative conversations, especially when I asked the person I was interviewing to clarify information. I had to learn to trust that when I was confused, it was because the information was confusing, not because I couldn't figure things out.

I became more confident in my ability to interview and felt as if I was improving. But I experienced highs and lows. Once, when there was something the newsroom needed to cover—but all of the reporters were out on assignments—someone suggested that an intern be sent to do it. I was sitting close enough to hear the conversation, and someone said they should send me to ask questions behind the scenes. One of the managers looked over at me, shook his head, and continued with the conversation. There went my confidence. Had he seen one of my interviews and thought I was terrible? At the time, I was trying to grow out a chemical relaxer, a process used on my hair since the fourth grade, so I looked a mess some days as I tried to find new professional styles for my kinky hair. I never mentioned that moment to anyone. I just kept working. (That manager appears later in my story, and that time he won't be shaking his head.)

Having an On-Camera Presence

Being on camera looks easy. It seems as if reporters and anchors are *just* reading or *just* talking, so I couldn't believe how hard it was to be myself in front of the camera. Some parts of the broadcasting world did feel natural to me. I have an outgoing personality, so talking to people was never difficult. I was not shy about jumping in front of the camera. But I did not walk into my internship TV ready. I was superawkward, as most people are, when I got in front of the camera, but I wasn't too worried. I had heard many of the greats, such as Soledad, talk about how she didn't start out with amazing skill.

There were so many distractions in the field: rain, extreme heat that made me sweat profusely, crowds of people at a crime scene, police sirens. And, of course, the camera draws a lot of attention, so people are staring too. I participated in theater in high school, which gave me an edge in being on camera, but there was still a lot I needed to work on. I would use this serious voice to project what I thought a news anchor should sound like when I should have focused on sounding like myself. I hated listening to myself speak when I played back pieces on tape—a bad sign. I sounded high pitched and unnatural. On top of that, sometimes my New Orleans accent popped out.

I meet many aspiring journalists in New Orleans who ask me how to get rid of their heavy accents. It's possible. I knew a reporter who sounded as if she was straight off of a farm in real life, but on TV, there was no trace of her country accent. Off camera, I have speech patterns typical of a New Orleanian. I say "zink" instead of "sink." I chop off the ends of words and speak too quickly. Sometimes, I speak in a way that's grammatically incorrect, knowing it's wrong. But when the camera comes on, I turn it off (most of the time). Speech coaches can help those who want to manage their accents. I didn't use one because I didn't have an intense accent. Also as part of my training, I watched Soledad's newscasts and noticed the pacing of her speech and her pronunciation of words. My on-camera presence is something I am always working on. Sometimes, I still speak too quickly, and if I get too comfortable, that New Orleans accent pops up again.

The crazy thing is that one person would tell me I sounded very "New Orleans" and needed to work on my accent, while another would tell me I had no accent. So many people in different disciplines gave me feedback as I worked to improve my on-camera presence. Broadcast news is a very subjective business. Each person I asked gave me different feedback. Since I was getting so much advice, I had to learn when to make changes and when to ignore the guidance. If I had taken all of the advice people gave me, I would have been running around like a chicken with its head cut off. So I listened to everything, but in the end, I had to use my own judgment.

Building a Résumé Tape

To apply for reporting jobs, I needed more than a paper resume. Aspiring reporters need a résumé reel, which is a tape that shows the reporter's work on air. To apply for producing jobs, I would need some samples of my writing or a tape of segments and stories that I had produced. Early on, I hadn't been sure of what I wanted to do, so I explored both on- and off-air positions. By the end of my internship, I knew for sure I preferred reporting more than producing.

There was only one problem regarding the creation of my resume reel. I wasn't actually on TV yet, so I didn't really have any work. But I was interning. I could grab a microphone and photographer and pretend to report all day, have the photographer record it, and then use that work to show that I had the potential to be a reporter. I put together several different résumé tapes while interning. They were terrible and filled with all the classic rookie mistakes. I tried too hard to sound like a "serious news person." I read and memorized lines instead of delivering and really thinking about the story I was telling. However, everyone who looked at my work told me I was pretty good. I hated listening to my stories because I didn't like how my voice sounded. I figured it was ok, or people would have told me that it wasn't.

Appearance

The tape is supposed to look like a real reporter put it together, so I kept my hair and makeup "TV ready" on the days I was shooting pieces for the tape. Preparing the reel offered an opportunity to practice putting on TV makeup and seeing how it looked on camera. TV makeup has to be a bit heavier than everyday makeup because all of the lights in the studio typically make people look washed out. I wish that it did not matter what I looked like, and that I could just focus on doing a good job. Sadly, that's just not the way this business works. Looks play a huge role. I had to look the part to land the part.

Stand-Ups

My tape began with four to five stand-ups, in which a reporter stands in front of the camera and gives a short bit of information that would move a story forward. Each one was fifteen to twenty seconds long and very visual. For instance, I would stand in front of a home that had been majorly damaged in a fire. I made sure that I was walking or demonstrating in some of them, to add a little action to the shots.

Packages

After the stand-ups, I needed three packages, which is just the news term for stories. A story is made up of pieces of video, sound bites (also referred to as SOTs, short for "sound on tape), which are just pieces of interviews with someone a reporter has spoken with, and a track of my voice telling the story. I was supposed to show that I was a strong writer and innovative storyteller.

What News Directors Look For

In evaluating applicants, news directors look at on-camera presence and potential. My potential news directors would know from my résumé that I didn't have real experience on camera, but I wanted to make my tape as strong as possible. I wish I could say that my tape made me look like an amazing reporter, but it didn't. Someone would have to look really hard to see that I had potential. The reality is that I was limited by my school schedule and only had so much time to get it done. My tape was cliché: fires, shootings, store openings. My mentor told me to aim for better stories, but by the end of my internship, those were the best I had—so that's what I went with. After all of that work and strategizing, my tape was terrible, but I didn't know it at the time. The most important thing was that I had finished it. After completing my first tape, I got right back to work on a new and improved one. I knew it could only get better from there.

6

It Takes More Than Skills!

Winners are not afraid of losing. But losers are. Failure is part of the process of success. People who avoid failure also avoid success.

Robert Kiyosaki, *Rich Dad, Poor Dad*

I was a woman on a mission. I use the word "woman" loosely. I felt like a child—a lost child—just trying to find my way out of the woods. I figured if I just kept walking forward, I would find my way eventually. I hustled as hard as I could during my internship, and even that wasn't enough to ensure that I would land a job in the news industry and thrive. Being successful is not just about working hard or being able to perform a checklist of skills. Hard work and skills are just the starting point. There were many interns at stations across the nation who had picked up the same skills. Some still managed to stand out over others—like two people having the same ingredients to make fried chicken and yet their chicken still tastes different. Just because I had the same skills—or less or more skills— as other job applicants, doesn't mean we were all the same. I think I stood out because of some qualities that aren't mentioned on a résumé. My attitude and the way I carried myself probably did a lot more to help me get ahead than any of the things I learned. Let's remember: My actual work was still pretty terrible.

Recovering from Mistakes

Interning in a news station is not a cruise-along kind of gig. I can remember feeling awkward, uncomfortable, and out of place so many times. But that feeling was a good thing. It meant that I was going outside of my comfort zone and putting myself out there while knowing that I might mess up.

Oh, and I did. Once, a high-profile anchor for the station let me help her with a story she was working on. The man in the story was a member of the military, and I used the wrong title when referring to him. She went on air and read the incorrect title. I can still feel the shame as if it just happened. The tens of thousands of viewers watching also had gotten the wrong information because of me. I learned an important lesson. Read and reread. It's the little things that matter when it comes to being accurate, and in news, accuracy is nonnegotiable. Don't focus on flowery language. Get the facts right!

I made lots of little mistakes. It was a waste of time to beat myself up for not being perfect. I don't know anyone who learned to ride a bike without falling off at least once. Making mistakes didn't mean that I wouldn't be a great journalist one day. I learned from each of my mistakes and moved on. When necessary, I apologized and then stopped dwelling on it. Hey, there were more mistakes to be made. If I didn't understand what I did wrong or how to avoid the situation in the future, I simply asked for guidance.

The great thing about being an intern is that I was expected to ask questions and not know stuff. I took full advantage of this. I knew that if everything went according to my plan, just a few months after being an intern, I could be working in a newsroom. I did not want to ask my questions when I was a paid employee who was supposed to know what she was doing. No one sees an intern as a threat. Almost everyone I work with now is focused on making us better as an organization, so on the whole, we help each other out. But in general, people are more willing to help an intern, as opposed to another reporter who should be at the same skill level.

When I practiced being on camera, I would certainly stumble and have to redo parts of my stories. I didn't feel so bad when I noticed that the seasoned reporters occasionally stumbled over words too. I learned from watching them that I just had to recover and start over. How I practiced would be how I delivered. I see many interns who make a big deal every time they trip over a word. They completely stop talking, giggle to make light of the situation, or keep apologizing. None of that is acceptable on live TV, so I didn't want to get into the habit of doing it when I practiced. Newsroom staff who I thought had never seen my work would compliment me or give me feedback after I practiced in front of the camera. I never knew who was watching, and I didn't want to freak out over a mistake in front of someone who happened to catch me practicing. Because stand-ups are recorded before the reporter is on air, reporters often tape stand-ups several times, until they do one that they feel good about. If they messed up during a live shot, they had to recover on air. Even though I wasn't live, I would keep talking no matter how bad I messed up and then I would do a better version, trying not to mess up at all.

Building a Professional Wardrobe

It would be great if a person's work just spoke for itself and people didn't have to be concerned about superficial things such as clothing or hair, but appearance does matter in this business. And women get the worst of it. Every woman I work with could show you countless emails with comments about her attire or hair or body. It's frustrating because our attire has no impact on our ability to deliver the news, and men are not judged on such superficial criteria. However, looks matter in TV. They are not everything, but presentation goes a long way.

This is a field where dressing for the job you want and not the one you have is very important. Newsrooms are very casual environments for people not working on TV. Everything—including jeans, sweatshirts, and flip-flops—is okay. Some interns came in looking as though they had just rolled out of bed. Their excuse was that they wanted to be producers, so they were not interested in being on camera. But I always dressed professionally. Doing so helped send the message that I was taking the opportunity seriously, but it also helped because I never knew where I would end up going each day. It was not abnormal to be sent out with a reporter and photographer to cover a funeral or event where everyone was dressed professionally.

One day, there was a small plane crash in the city. Since I was properly dressed, I was able to do a stand-up. Something like that doesn't happen often. When it came to wardrobe, I was always ready. There are people who go overboard and show up with a full suit, heels, and makeup every day. However, a nice top and pants or skirt, with sensible heels or nice flats, is perfect. There were times I needed to help with camera equipment, and I would just look silly if I had stilettos on. I also started noticing what looked good on camera. Sometimes, I would think an outfit was really cute, but when I watched it back on screen, it wasn't flattering. As a general rule, solid, bright colors and jewel tones look good on TV. Small prints don't usually translate well on camera.

I was still in college, so I didn't have a lot of money to spend on a professional wardrobe. I became a master of mixing and matching. Some simple basics got me through until I had a job with enough money to spend a little bit on clothing:

- black blazer
- black pencil skirt or black pants
- tank tops of different colors
- solid-colored dresses and tops

I still mix and match these basics to stretch my wardrobe, so that I do not spend all of my money on clothing. I also do a lot of shopping at thrift stores. Back then I was being young and dumb, thinking I was too cool for the thrift store. Now, I proudly march in and dig until I uncover some great five-dollar finds. When I interned, I felt most comfortable when I stuck with my own everyday style but translated it into a professional look. I don't feel comfortable in dress pants, but at first, I bought a ton and would wear them because I thought that's what professionals wore. Eventually, I realized I wasn't missing anything by not wearing them. A black pencil skirt is a lifesaver for me to this day. I had one skirt—which cost less than thirty dollars and fit me amazingly—that I was wearing several times a week with different tops and blazers, and no one noticed. No one can tell one black skirt from another. I am a fan of clothing deals, and for the most part, it's hard to tell on TV if something is cheaply made, which is great because sometimes anchors and reporters won't wear the same dress very often if it has a memorable pattern.

I know it's annoying to put that much thought into clothing, but the reality is I had to because appearance plays a huge role in how TV personalities are perceived by viewers. As for makeup, I hardly ever wore it before I was on TV. Thankfully, I had used it enough for high school plays to be somewhat familiar with what I was doing. My application still wasn't very good though. I picked up tips over the years through buying makeup products in the mall and then asking the makeup artists in the store to apply it for me, watching tutorials online, and paying attention when makeup artists did my face.

Hair

My hair has proven to be one of the biggest struggles of my career in journalism. In its natural state, my hair looks like the singer Chaka Khan's hair. That was actually my nickname in early middle school, before I got a relaxer to permanently straighten my hair. By the time I started interning, I had been wanting to grow the relaxer out for years, but it was difficult. When I was building my résumé tape, I was trying for the hundredth time to grow out the chemical relaxer that had been put in my hair since I was in fourth grade.

When I was an intern, the few inches of my hair at the root were made up of the natural kinky wavy hair that comes out of my head. The rest was chemically straightened hair that looked stringy in comparison to my naturally thick locks. I didn't want short hair, so I experimented with styles to blend the two types of hair together. On many days, I looked a mess. I taped some of my pieces for my résumé reel with a curly afro, but eventually some of the people who worked at the news station started suggesting that I straighten it to land a job. I was annoyed but grateful for their honesty. I have seen a few black women in news rock their natural hair on TV, but it's often very short. I have kinky hair that reaches the middle of my back and grows larger and larger in the New Orleans humidity. I haven't seen that rocked on TV news yet.

I wanted to do so, but I couldn't afford not to be hired because of my hair. An employer wasn't going to admit that they weren't hiring me because my hair was all over the place. I just wouldn't get a call. I have decided to conform until I get further along in my career, but even conforming isn't easy. My hair is completely natural now, but I use a mixture of weaves, wigs, and buns to keep it looking straight for TV. And, honestly, I hate it. I love my hair—my real natural, crazy hair. I never—and I mean not even once—wore fake hair before I got on TV. And for the first few years, I still refused to, but I was breaking my hair off trying to straighten it multiple times a day to look TV ready at all times. When young women with kinky curly hair ask me for advice on the hair front, I tell them the same thing: Straighten it until you get to a comfortable place in your career. I hope one day that advice won't be necessary, and we'll see big kinky afros all over network news.

Attitude

I had school assignments that were related to my internship, and I had a checklist of internship tasks to accomplish. But let's be real, no one really cared what I got out of my internship. UNO would not have been any worse off if I didn't learn anything. The news station wasn't depending on me to get anything done. In school, there were always tests and teachers who made sure I met certain standards. In the real world, it was up to me to challenge myself—for myself. I never wasted time on social media or sat around goofing off while I was at the news station, even though the staff would occasionally. The big difference was that the people who worked there already had a job. I needed one. If I had free time or felt bored, I felt I was not taking full advantage of my surroundings. There was so much to do that I could have been occupied the entire time I was there and still have more to learn. My internship was more of a personal journey. It was up to me to decide how much I got out of it. I told myself every day that I had everything to gain and nothing to lose, and that helped me to take initiative and talk to people I otherwise might not have.

It also helped to be someone people wanted to be around. Employees are not forced to work with interns. So they avoid people who are annoying, lazy, and obnoxious. Now that I am on the other side of the table, I think the most annoying thing an intern can do is come in with the attitude that they know everything. And when I was an intern, I had to get used to hearing criticism without being defensive. I didn't agree with everyone who gave me feedback, but I was appreciative that they were even taking the time to talk to me about my future and about improving myself. If I didn't agree, I just said thanks.

Sacrifice

When I was still fighting my way through college, some things I did were just about making a little money, like the retail job I had. I had no aspirations of working in retail. I was making t-shirts. Those skills wouldn't help me in my career path. My internships were the gigs that I needed to further my career, but they were not paid. Thankfully, more and more places now require that interns be paid. I did receive college credit for my internships, which means they replaced one of my classes. And trust me, they were much more valuable than any class I ever took.

Many of the amazing opportunities available to an up-and-coming journalist are unpaid gigs. The truth is that I really couldn't afford to work for free. But nothing comes without sacrifice. There are some paid opportunities for entry-level journalists. Some people work as desk assistants in newsrooms, answering phones and running scripts. Another entry-level option is camera operator. Camera operators put the studio cameras in the right position to frame the anchors. But those jobs don't typically pay much (we're talking eight to ten dollars an hour).

I do think interns in all fields should be paid, to level the playing field. Unpaid internships make it easier for privileged young people to succeed over those with less financial resources. Some people have to support themselves and their families while they are in college, so they pass up opportunities where they won't be compensated. I was able to make it work thanks to my parents, who continued to sacrifice to help support me. I was not working when I interned at CNN, because I couldn't find anyone who would hire me for just a month in the summer. Soledad helped by paying me for odd jobs, such as babysitting her nieces. While I interned at WDSU in New Orleans, I worked side jobs with Kim.

I struggled financially while balancing an internship and a full-time school schedule, but I got a lot more out of my internship, since I did not have to limit my time at the station because of another job. I was able to be there before classes and on weekends. Is it fair that some people have their parents to turn to in a bind and others are on their own financially? No, but whining about it won't help. I knew that I would have to make it through a time when opportunities were not financially lucrative. What I missed out on in cash in the short term, I gained in experience that propelled me to where I am today.

Making Connections

I hate the idea of networking. Getting to know people just because they have some benefit to my life or career seems fake. But during my internship, I did end up building meaningful relationships without sucking up to people. Each person in the newsroom who I built a relationship with was someone I genuinely wanted to talk to. As is the case everywhere, there were some people in the newsroom who I didn't particularly like working with. The great thing is there are other people. I gravitated toward the people who I related to and could have real conversations with. That way, it was more natural when I had a question about something work related.

An easy way to test the waters with everyone in the newsroom was to introduce myself and ask what they were working on. Sometimes, they politely blew me off because they were busy, but usually they would reach out later. More often than not, they were open to a conversation, and I would ask them what they are responsible for doing every day.

Offering to help was a great way to bond naturally. I made friends with a lot of reporters by logging interviews for them. Afterward, I had a relationship with that person, and I felt comfortable asking them to read over scripts or look at some of my stand-ups. When someone asked me to do something for them, I did it. I didn't always get something out of it at that exact moment. But it made it easier for me to go back to them and ask for guidance, because I already had a relationship with them.

Although I liked Gina a lot from the beginning, I didn't want to get attached to one person too quickly. I wanted to get to know as many people as possible. The people in the newsroom were all possible future job connections. So the more of them I knew, the better.

7

Mentoring

A candle loses nothing by lighting another candle.

James Keller

I consider myself an independent person, but I never let that stop me from asking for help or admitting that I didn't know something. The connections I was making would eventually help me advance in the business, and finding a mentor was a game changer for me. It was invaluable to have people in my field who answered my questions and showed me the ropes. The questions didn't stop the minute I landed a job. I just had new questions and new obstacles to navigate.

What Mentoring Looks Like

I had never looked for a mentor. My first mentor was my college professor, Kim, but I didn't think of her as my mentor until years after we met. I thought of her as my professor at first and then my friend. Our relationship developed over time. Kim and I first had conversations about concepts covered in class, and from there, we ended up talking about ourselves and our lives. We became friends, and I started asking more questions about working in the news industry and how she got started. Kim left CNN as a vice president to move back to New Orleans and help the city and her family rebuild after Katrina. The more she talked to me about what it was like to work in a newsroom and how she got there, the more I felt as if I could do it too.

After my CNN internship in New York, I came back to New Orleans to finish my senior year. Kim was done with graduate school and teaching, and was starting her own production company. She had several gigs to plan events around the city, and she hired me as her assistant. I was working a dead-end job at a college store making T-shirts, working events with Kim, and taking classes. Midterm exams served as a major wake-up call that I had taken on too much. I bombed one exam, and in that class, there was only one other test for the entire semester. I was overwhelmed, and I knew that something had to go. Kim encouraged me to leave the retail job, since it wasn't getting me any closer to where I wanted to be. She helped me keep regular work as her assistant on production gigs and provided me with many other connections that led to freelance work. I was writing scripts for events and helping with event planning. That was the thing about Kim. She didn't just encourage me to make the leap. She made it possible.

Kim and I had very serious conversations about my future, and she wasn't afraid to give me her honest opinion about anything. Even though I worked as her assistant, we also had a lot of fun together. We would go to restaurants, go shopping, watch movies—normal things friends do. She also let me into her network, allowing me to make connections with other successful women. I could go on and on about all that she has done for me, and I still would not be able to convey how she changed my life.

Soledad also treated me like a friend, even when I was her intern. She flew me to Miami to speak at a fundraiser with music mogul Pharrell Williams. She flies me to New York every summer for an amazing weekend with the other scholars of PowHERful Foundation, an event to empower young women. And now that I have graduated from that program, she continues to give me great opportunities. I interview celebrities at her functions, and I have been the keynote speaker at the annual event in New York. She also flies me all over the country to emcee empowerment conferences for her PowHERful Foundation. I can still email her in the middle of the night about any problem I am having, and she is always ready to brainstorm a solution. Mentoring doesn't always look like a stale quarterly meeting. It's a relationship and an exchange of knowledge, but I was very lucky, because for me those relationships turned into friendships.

It's Not about Being Perfect

When I met Kim and Soledad, they were superwomen to me: successful, intelligent, confident, down to earth, funny, and flawless. They both looked fabulous while getting so much done. I wanted to be just like them. Every time I told Soledad how amazing I thought she was, she revealed a practical trick behind what seemed like magic to me. "How do you maintain your schedule with four kids?" Nannies, she'd say. "How do you find time to cook?" I don't. "How did you get where you are today?" Hard work. She wasn't getting everything done perfectly. She had a lot of help to pull it off, and sometimes things fell through the cracks. The more I got to know her, the more I realized that her power did not come from being flawless. It was just the opposite. Her power came from how she dealt with her shortcomings and how honest she was about them. When she explained that she had a lot of help, it made me feel okay about needing help too.

Soledad once told a group of young girls that she was never the most gorgeous woman around, but it didn't matter, because she was working hard. We all thought she was crazy. But now I understand what she was trying to say. Her accomplishments are not a result of her being exceptionally smart or attractive. And thank God, I couldn't have found much inspiration in that, because I couldn't change how smart or attractive I was. I have always been fascinated by the idea that the prettiest, most talented, or smartest people aren't always the most successful. Instead, we think of them as pretty or talented or smart because of where they are. How many famous and extremely successful singers can we name who are criticized for their vocal talents? We all know someone from around the corner who can sing way better, but they aren't in the same position. Soledad was focused on the factors that she could control, such as how hard she worked. She showed me that I could be more successful than the prettiest or smartest person in the room if I put in more effort.

Finding a Mentor

I had amazing parents, but I couldn't turn to them for advice about the professional world. My mom always said that she explained her mistakes to me so that I didn't have to make the same ones. My mentors did the same thing, sharing their stories of regrets, failures, and lessons learned so that I could walk through similar experiences with more knowledge and perspective than they had. I certainly wasn't the first young woman who was interested in journalism but had no idea where to start. I didn't have to figure it all out through trial and error. Soledad and Kim were there to help me avoid some of the obstacles they had encountered.

I had already found my mentors by the time I started interning, but an internship is a great place to find a mentor. There are some definite don'ts in looking for one. I have about a dozen people I consider mentors, but I've never asked anyone to be my mentor. And I don't think anyone ever should ask that question. It's awkward. It would be like walking up to a cute guy and asking him to be my boyfriend. Relationships have to develop naturally and that takes time. There was no way to know the first time I spoke to someone that they would make a great mentor for me.

There are a few other no-nos when it comes to finding a mentor. Never ask anyone how much money they make. It seems obvious, but I get asked this question all the time. Even for people who want to be in the business, knowing a specific anchor or reporter's salary isn't relevant, because news industry salaries depend on market, position, experience, and many other factors. A more useful question for an aspiring journalist to ask would be, "How much money does an entry-level reporter, anchor, etc., make in this market?" I never asked anyone directly how much they made, but as I built relationships, I had reliable sources who could help me figure out how much I should be making. I ended up making friends with a producer, and after I had shadowed that position for some time, we developed a relationship. She started talking to me about her salary without me even asking. I think she wanted to give me a heads-up about what I was getting myself into. My mentors were very helpful in determining if I was being given a fair offer in my first contract, since I had nothing to compare it to.

Also, when approaching possible mentors, I didn't want to be annoying. Mentors are busy people. They have jobs, real-life responsibilities, and sometimes families, and they were trying to help me. I loved to talk with my mentors over email. That way, they were not pressured to answer before they had time. Too many texts or phone calls can be overwhelming. I didn't want to become a burden to them.

Ask Questions

Asking questions is an easy way to form a connection that could possibly turn into a mentoring relationship. This tactic also works at any stage of the game. Kim and I became close because I always had questions for her and she was eager to answer them. When I interned at CNN, sometimes making a connection was as simple as asking someone what they were responsible for doing every day. It was an easy and natural way to kick-start a conversation and let the person know that I was interested.

I didn't just ask questions about work. I wanted to get to know them, too, as people outside of work, without being invasive. On a shoot at CNN, I talked to one of the senior producers about her daughter, and with one of the cameramen about his trips to New Orleans. Talking to them about their lives made it easier to turn to them in the future if I ever need help with anything.

If I run into someone outside of a work setting and I think they could be helpful to my career, I ask for their email address and leave it at that. I never want to disrupt someone's personal time.

Offer to Help

Another way to find a mentor is by offering to help. I would ask producers and reporters—actually, anyone—in the newsroom what I could do to help. I would offer to log scripts, carry equipment, or do research. Doing this showed that I wanted to work and be helpful. I found that the easiest way to get to know someone was to help them with something. Then when that person needed help again, they would already be familiar with me.

Find a Connection

I was very lucky to meet a lot of really nice people who were more than happy to help me along my journey, but I never officially labeled them all mentors. I would compare it to being in a classroom of people but considering only some of them your friends. I knew when I had found a potential mentor, because I felt comfortable asking them for advice. The conversations felt genuine, and the connection gradually evolved into a lasting relationship. It was just like meeting someone I "clicked" with the first time we met, but the relationship still had to develop for a while before I called them a friend. Mentoring is the same way. It takes time to see if there is potential for a lasting relationship with the person.

I asked everyone I came across for advice. Some of the relationships with those advice givers lasted, and others didn't. Some people were only able to offer advice and help through one part of my journey. There are so many people who have helped me with one assignment or task, such as putting my first résumé tape together. They were all mentors in a sense, but I wasn't focused on titles. I was too busy trying to soak up knowledge from as many people around me as I could. I call Kim and Soledad my mentors because we have ongoing relationships that evolved over time, but at the base of the relationship, they are always there for support and guidance—while many other people had helped me with one particular issue and the relationship didn't really have any more depth to it than that. If I would have been distracted by the search for the perfect mentor, I would have missed out on a lot of great information from other people who helped me along the way.

8

Landing the First Job

Life is a series of steps. Things are done gradually. Once in a while there is a giant step, but most of the time we are taking small, seemingly insignificant steps on the stairway of life.

Ralph Ransom

Using My Connections

By May 2011, my internship at WDSU was coming to an end, and I was preparing to graduate. I hadn't had any interactions with the news director or general manager at WDSU, but Kim suggested that I set up a meeting with each of them. I did and thanked them for the experience. I also asked them to keep me in mind if any positions opened. I had such a great experience interning there and, at the time, really wanted them to hire me. That station did eventually reach out to discuss hiring me, but by that time, I was working on my career at WWL.

As the internship ended, I sent my résumé tape out to stations all over the country and got zero calls back. I had heard from many successful journalists, including Soledad, that it was a tough process and could take a while to get a call back. So I didn't panic. Graduation came and went, and I still hadn't gotten any responses about my tape. Kim had moved on to other projects, but she had helped me meet so many great people while we worked together that I had no problem finding a job. I started working with an event production company that Kim introduced me to. The company had a contract to produce the Bayou Classic football game and events. The game is a huge annual showdown between two Louisiana HBCUs (historically black colleges and universities): Grambling State University and Southern University and A&M College. I helped with event coordination. The job involved lots of great opportunities, but it definitely was not for me. Event production requires a lot of attention to detail, and let's be real, some days I have to look down to

89

remember what color I'm wearing. Event planners also have to keep their clients happy, and I found it annoying to have to appease people for a living. Thankfully, I was working for a great woman, Dottie Belletto, who knew that my real dream was to work in the news.

Dottie owns a company that produces programs and events. She has nothing to do with the news, but she's been a great encourager in my career—before it even existed. We still keep in touch. She gives me great feedback on my projects. Plus, she is superconnected in the city and has helped me build some great relationships in the community. She has helped me in so many ways. She even hired my little brother when he needed some work experience and was home from college. And she just cares about my future success. It's been beneficial to have mentor-like figures outside of my direct field, because it's great to have a trusted perspective that is different. Dottie has been one of my main cheerleaders from day one, and she supported my dream even though it meant leaving her company.

By the end of the summer, I had applied to so many jobs that I was barely keeping track anymore. I just needed one news station to return my call. And eventually one did. It was WWL. I was in the office, working on the Bayou Classic, when the phone rang. On the line was one of my now executive producers asking if I was still interested in an associate producer position. I had applied for it months ago. A friend of Kim's who worked at WWL had promised to pass my résumé along. But in a situation similar to when I tried to intern at WWL, I had never gotten any response. I figured my résumé had never even made it there, and if it did, it was in the trash somewhere. But on the call, I agreed to interview, and I immediately told Kim and Soledad I needed to be ready.

The Interview

Kim and Soledad jumped right into action. They sent me cheat sheets of things to know—all the city council members, the biggest stories going on at the time—and stories from their first interviews and how they answered questions. I stayed up late reading the news until I could recite it without a teleprompter. And of course, I was overly prepared. My interviewers didn't ask me anything about the news. Instead, they gave me a writing test. I was given three stories from the Associated Press wires. I had ten minutes to turn them into broadcast stories. It was the same task Gina made me do every day during my WDSU internship. I did it without sweating. Was this really going to be it? I chatted with two of my now executive producers before I was brought into the news director's office, where all of the managers had gathered to assess me.

It was my first real interview. I was in a room full of men, and I was not familiar with any of them. It was intimidating. All eyes were on me, and I felt as if I was overanalyzing every word that came out of my mouth. They asked me about myself, and I told them my experience being from New Orleans, leaving NYU, and going to UNO; about finishing school; and loving to write. I remember being asked more than once if I wanted to be on camera. I was hesitant to tell them about my dreams of being on camera because the job I was applying for did not involve being on camera. I said that I wanted to be an associate producer so that I could work on writing and maybe in a few years transition to on-camera work. Then, I told them my ultimate goal: hosting my own talk show. One executive producer, Dominic Massa, who is one of my favorite people now, replied, "Everyone wants their own show." I immediately regretted saying it and figured I had blown it. I don't remember what they asked me after that. In Dominic's defense, there's no way he remembers telling me that. He has no idea that I still have nightmares about it (just kidding). Dominic has a very quirky sense of humor that I didn't get at all back then. Today he is one of my favorite people to go to for a laugh, one of my biggest cheerleaders (well without the actual hoorahs and cheering—that wouldn't be very Dominic-like), and part of the foundation of WWL.

A few days passed, and I heard through the grapevine that I was one of the final contenders for the job, along with another woman who had worked at *Today*. I wish that I could say I was still confident that I had a chance, but I underestimated myself. I figured I couldn't possibly stand a chance against someone who had already worked in the industry for a national show, when I had never even had a real paying job in TV news.

Within the week, however, I got the call saying the job was mine. After all those months of waiting, this was it. I was an associate producer at WWL. It sounds amazing, right? It *was* amazing that I found a job at home in my field of choice, and I had my "in." But the job definitely wasn't as prestigious as the title sounds. Let me break it down.

Job title: Associate Producer, WWL-TV
Full time or part time: Part time
Hours: 2:00 a.m. – 7:00 a.m.
Wages: $10/hour

My point is I still had a long way to go. I didn't have any money saved, and

I still had $60,000 in school-related debt. I kept the job at the event-planning company. It was only a few blocks away from WWL. My day started at two o'clock in the morning, and I went in even earlier than that because I was new and needed extra time to get my work done. After my shift at the station, I would head over to the event-planning company, where I was supposed to work until midday. At the event-planning company, I was the lead in organizing a college and career fair for the Bayou Classic. As the date for the event got closer, that goal of leaving the office at midday disappeared. I was there late into the evenings, getting home with just enough time to nap before going to WWL. When I think back on that time, I remember being so insanely focused on getting everything done that I pushed aside any reasonable feelings of fatigue and kept moving. I was so grateful to have gotten the job at WWL.

Being an Associate Producer

Associate producers help write scripts for the show. There's so much to write to make a newscast happen and only so much time to get it done. The job was very stressful. There wasn't much training before I started writing for the show. I had to learn the hard way that there is no such thing as not getting it done.

One morning, I was working on a story, thinking out each word carefully. I felt as though I was moving really fast, but I was getting only about one story done in the time it took the seasoned producers to do ten. They kept asking if I was done with my story. I was getting overwhelmed and started panicking. My executive producer said it was time for the anchors to read the story. There was chaos as the other producers tried to communicate to the anchors and directors that the story was not done. That was the last time they ever looked for a story from me that I had not finished. I may have been part time and not making a lot of money, but I realized then how critical my job was to getting people the news they needed in the morning.

Producing or Reporting?

Being an associate producer was a great opportunity, but I did not see myself as a producer in the long-term. There were aspects of producing that I loved. I liked writing and finding content for shows, but not the pressure. I had to write quickly. I hated the constant feeling that I could have written a script better or been more concise had there been enough time. The station was giving me more opportunities to grow as a producer, but I knew it wasn't for me. Even on my best day, during my shift, I felt anxious about not being able to finish everything on time. I also didn't enjoy rewording stories provided in press releases or wires.

Reporters actually gather facts and eyewitness accounts. Reporters decide what part of a story is told and who tells it. Producers are responsible for everyone in the show and for making sure things run smoothly. Reporters just make sure their one story is done. Producers tend to be detail-oriented people. They have to make sure the proper graphics and spellings accompany each story. Reporters are responsible only for their scripts.

I definitely benefited from being an associate producer. My writing was much stronger than when I started, and I saw the business from a different role than the one I ultimately wanted, which just enhanced my perspective. I understand what producers want from reporters, and that influenced how I operated once I became a reporter. For instance, reporters have to let producers know what words they will say before video should start playing or before a certain graphic appears. Those words are called roll cues. I saw how tough it was when reporters sent those cues to producers only moments before going live, so I always try to send mine as soon as possible.

Being a Producer Didn't Qualify Me to Be a Reporter

Many young journalists wonder if they should produce before they report. I did, and so did my mentors. I wanted to go straight into reporting, but no one wanted to hire me. Working as a producer helped me be a better writer, but it couldn't help me prepare to be on air. As a producer, I was not working on my on-camera presence, delivery, or tone of voice. Still, even though I didn't get that reporting job first, I was in a newsroom, and I had access to resources that would help me get where I wanted to be. But even if a reporting position opened, I would be up against people who had been at other stations working on their reporting skills. I needed experience on air, and to get that, I would need to go to a smaller market, where it was easier for inexperienced reporters to be hired. I never even thought about being hired by WWL to be on air. Some of the other aspiring reporters waited behind the scenes to get their big break from someone getting stuck in traffic and not making it to work, but I knew that wasn't realistic. Even if that happened, some other on-air talent would fill in for the missing person.

If I had had my way, I would have gone straight into a reporting job in a smaller market. I had never realized how easy it was to get comfortable in a place I didn't even want to be. I have met many people who had ambitious goals and planned to switch positions, but it seemed they let those dreams fizzle out over time. And that's understandable.

It would be easy for me to pick up and switch stations because I had no reason to stay in New Orleans. I wasn't in a serious relationship at the time. I didn't have any kids. I didn't own a home. I was commitment free. I figured I could go to a small town, get two years of experience, and then move to somewhere I wanted to be—all before I was twenty-five. I knew that as I got older, "life" would happen, and I would have more reasons not to chase my dreams. Even with nothing holding me back, the idea of such a big change was still hard for me. I was getting used to working my two jobs and was losing some of the initial fire I had to get a reporting job. But there is always anxiety when it comes to doing something new. Waiting would not make the leap any easier, so I thought I might as well get it over with sooner rather than later.

Learning to Be Uncomfortable

At some point, it clicked for me that I could not avoid being uncomfortable. After being at WWL a few months, I didn't think that I was making the most of my time there. I was working at the event planning company, and though it was time consuming, I wanted to keep the money. But advancing my career was more important than getting a check for something I ultimately didn't want to do. I told Dottie I would stay on to finish out the Bayou Classic, and then I would work only at the news station. When the Bayou Classic was over, I could finally spend my free time working on my résumé reel. I would go out with the weekend reporter to do stand-ups, and I would use the video and sound from packages that reporters had done during the week to write my own stories.

I let anyone who would give me the time of day watch what I was working on and give me feedback, but it was Mike Hoss, who would end up being my co-anchor, who gave me game-changing advice. He told me that my voice was high pitched and I needed to talk more like I did in everyday life. He suggested I take scripts into the audio booth and keep reading them and listening to the tapes until I could control my voice better. After a few weeks, I was drastically improving. I kept adding new clips to my résumé reel, and the tape was way better than the first one I made while interning.

Mike wasn't helping just me. He was also helping the other young woman who had been a candidate with me for the associate producer position. She had been hired in the position beneath mine. Not long after Mike started helping her, she was reporting on the evening news and doing live shots. We were about the same age, we had been hired at the same time, and Mike was helping us both. He had chosen her to be on TV. I remember sharing with Soledad and Kim that I couldn't stop wondering why the station had chosen her over me. Soledad told me a story about a woman she had worked with at one point in her career. Soledad felt as if she was in the woman's shadow, but she just kept working hard and doing her thing. And eventually, she became successful, despite having felt that the woman had been in a better position than she was. I stayed focused on my goal, but I couldn't help thinking that the other hire must have been much better than I was, since she got to be on air and I didn't.

One day, a photographer with whom I had been working on the weekends said, "I thought you wanted to be a reporter."

"I did," I told him.

"Then what are you waiting for?" he replied. I didn't have a good answer. I didn't even have an okay answer. I told him that I wanted to save more money before I moved away, and I wanted to get better. He pointed out that there are people who come straight out of college and get reporting jobs. He insisted that I was good enough now and went to a computer to show me a job that was open in Lafayette, Louisiana, which was a little more than two hours away from New Orleans. It was a small market, so maybe I would have a chance.

I had been saying I wanted to be a reporter, but I hadn't applied for a new job in months. I was finally in my groove as an associate producer at WWL. My managers thought of me as a good writer. I was able to keep up with the pace of writing the morning show. I was settled. I had gotten comfortable, and there were so many little concerns nudging me away from my ultimate goal. There was the hesitation about moving without a lot of money, the fear of not being good enough, and the people around me telling me that I would be such a great producer so I shouldn't focus on reporting. In fact, the station was giving me more and more opportunities to fill in for producers when they were off and to produce shows by myself. I realized how easily I was getting off course without even noticing it. I wanted to make sure that if I did change my mind, I wasn't doing it out of fear or because of other people's opinions.

I wasn't making anywhere near enough money to support myself or pay back all of the loans I had accumulated in college. I was working two jobs. I was tired all the time, and yet I had started to get comfortable. It would have been easy to remain a producer because I already was one, not because

I was happy with it. Becoming a reporter would require a lot of effort, work, growing pains, and a new adjustment period.

I started thinking about all the people I knew who were unhappy with their jobs and could have explored other options but didn't. I looked at how the fear of uncertainty had paralyzed the people around me. The fear wasn't just about jobs. I thought of all my friends who were in unhappy relationships. So I asked myself, "Am I an associate producer because it's good for me professionally and it's what I really want or just because it is comfortable?" Everything I wanted was out of my comfort zone, because I had never done it. I would never get to the next level if I didn't force myself to be uncomfortable. Staying on my current path was like wanting to get to the top of a flight of stairs and never expecting to have to step higher. But I knew how to conquer discomfort. I always feel this hollow discomfort in my stomach when I have to speak in front of a large audience. The discomfort is temporary, and not long after I start speaking, I get into a groove and forget that feeling was ever there. In most situations, if I forced myself to be uncomfortable, eventually the discomfort faded away.

I wish that I could tell you I had that much clarity when the photographer asked me why I wasn't reporting yet. It wasn't until after I had moved on that I realized I was getting comfortable and not growing. I don't remember my exact thought process at that moment, but I do remember thinking that my photographer friend was right. As I thought about how much further ahead in my career I wanted to be, I was overcome by a sudden sense of urgency to get moving. I didn't have time to waste. It was like something inside me woke up and asked, "Sheba, if you don't feel ready now, when will you ever?" That little voice made a good point. It was time for me to get over the fact that I didn't feel ready and make the leap. I was afraid. I was nervous. I was too comfortable. I was all of these things that were just getting in the way of me being where I wanted to be. But I had to ignore all of the negative emotions and push forward. Taking a moment to stop and ask myself if I liked what I was doing—and, more importantly, where was I headed—was crucial to my career after those first months. I wanted to walk a different path than the one I was on. To do so, I would have to do something different.

9

Moving beyond the First Job

Begin with the end in mind.

Stephen Covey,
The 7 Habits of Highly Effective People

Focusing on the Big Picture

I set up a meeting with Bill Siegel, my news director. I thanked him for the opportunity to work at WWL, but I told him that I was certain I wanted to be a reporter. I explained that I would love to work at WWL in the future, but for now, I wanted to leave and find a reporting job. He offered to help me find one.

Before then, I don't remember having much of a relationship with Bill. It wasn't the easiest meeting, but I was extremely grateful that he had taken a gamble and hired me. So I didn't want to leave without saying thank you. I didn't want him to assume that I was leaving because I didn't like it or didn't want to work in the business. I wanted to make it very clear that I was happy working at WWL, but simply working at WWL wasn't good enough. I was willing to do anything to get where I wanted to be, even though it seemed I was taking a step back by leaving such a highly regarded station.

To be clear, I did not want to leave, but leaving seemed to be the best strategy for achieving my long-term vision. I didn't know it then, but being willing to sacrifice my immediate comfort to get my future on track would be crucial to reaching my goals. Life is always about the big picture. Growing up with so many financial struggles, my eye was always on the future. I knew that things were a mess, so I was always thinking about what I could do to make sure things would be different in the future. I unknowingly carried that attitude into the workforce. Being an associate producer was fine for the present, but if I didn't make any changes, it would also have been my future.

Bill said he would make some calls for me. I sent out my updated résumé tape and applied for jobs as often as I could. He updated me on his efforts too. Thanks to him, the job search wasn't a very long process. He called a news station in Baton Rouge, a market much smaller than New Orleans. He said the news director there had looked at my tape, but he didn't think I was ready for TV yet and thought I should try an even smaller market. Bill then called a station in Lafayette. The news director agreed to interview me that Friday.

I had applied to a job at another station in Lafayette before Bill had stepped in to help. Someone else suggested that I call that station and ask to speak to the person in charge. The job posting clearly said no calls, but I ignored it and called anyway. The news director answered and sternly kept repeating that the posting clearly said not to call. I apologized and hung up the phone. I felt so embarrassed and dumb. Why had I called when the posting said no calls! I told Bill that I was sure I had already blown it with the other station in Lafayette. He assured me that the news director there would never remember that phone call and that I should reach out again, since I would be in town. I never wanted to call that station again, but I did and asked if I could meet with someone to talk about any future openings.

I took a Friday off from work and drove to Lafayette in a friend's car. I was extremely nervous, but things went great. The news director was a really nice woman who gave me a lot of feedback on what I needed to work on, but I felt as if she liked me. Then I hopped across the street to meet with the man who had made me feel so terrible on the phone. Just as Bill had promised, he did not remember my name and didn't bring up my unwanted phone call. He said he didn't have any jobs open, but he would keep me in mind. No matter how things turned out, I was proud of myself for pushing past that uncomfortable feeling in my gut and going through with the interviews.

Faux Negotiating

Within a week, the first news director I had interviewed with in Lafayette called to say the job was mine. I couldn't believe that I finally had a reporting job. It paid $24,000 a year, and I would need to move to Lafayette within the month. I accepted. I was thrilled to tell Bill and thank him for his help. I will never forget his response: "Really? I didn't think you would get it." He hadn't been completely honest about how much work he thought I needed, but it was probably for the best, because I already wasn't a hundred percent confident in myself. He told me that he hadn't expected leaving to be an option for me so quickly, because he didn't think I would get a reporting job.

My plan had worked out, and just when I thought things couldn't have worked out better, Bill made me an offer that I never saw coming. He told me the traffic reporter position at WWL would be open soon, and he thought I should stay and apply for it. It was unreal. Here I was driving more than two hours away to look for a job, only to be offered one where I already was. It turns out, Bill hadn't reviewed my updated résumé reel until he knew I was leaving. When he finally did, he was impressed by how much progress I had made over just a few months.

My first thought was that the woman who had been hired with me would apply and she would be chosen over me, since she was already on air. It was as though Bill read my mind. He hinted that things weren't working out with that person, and that if I applied, he would consider me the front-runner at the station. I never would have imagined that I had any chance over her, because the newsroom seemed to favor her. I was glad I listened to Soledad and Kim and kept doing my thing.

Also, being a traffic reporter was not my dream job. I never fantasized about being on TV. I dreamed of doing great interviews and telling captivating stories. I wanted to be a field reporter. Bill understood my goals and convinced me to take the job anyway. First, it paid more than the job in Lafayette. On top of that, the Lafayette position would have required me to be a multimedia journalist, or MMJ. I would have had to shoot and edit my own pieces. Bill told me that I could do traffic for the morning show, from five o'clock until the show ended at nine, and then I could work on news stories with a traffic angle after the show.

I didn't feel comfortable negotiating my salary or career moves. I could have nodded yes, smiled, and thanked Bill for just letting me be on TV—but if I had done so, I don't think I'd be where I am today. I had to make myself have a very difficult conversation (they get easier!). I was extremely grateful that he had looked beyond my lack of experience and given me a chance, but I also needed to make sure I wasn't accepting a position that would deter me from my ultimate goal. Reporting traffic would not have prepared me for the job I actually wanted: reporting news. It was important to me that management shared my vision for my future. He could have said that he saw me only as a good traffic reporter, and then I would have known to move on to a place where the people around me supported my vision. Jobs are like relationships in many ways: an exchange. Managers need tasks done, and employees need opportunities for growth (and money, of course). Kim told me I had to make my needs clear from the beginning. Not doing so would be like wanting to be married but being with someone who didn't consider me marriage material. In that case, it would not be wise to stick around and try to convince him that I'd make a good wife. The logical option is to move on to someone who already sees that potential in me. I wanted the same support from my professional relationships. I wanted to work for someone who supported my vision and believed in me. I knew that it might take some time to convince the higher-ups in my organization to see what I saw in myself. But I also knew that if months or years later I was still trying to convince them to give me opportunities, it would be time to find a place that was willing to take a chance on me.

I told the news director in Lafayette that even though I had accepted the job, something had come up and I would be staying in New Orleans. She was livid. I guess she felt as if I had wasted her time. "I'm just going to tell you. Your news director said you weren't ready to be on TV," she said and hung up the phone. Not long after I accepted the position at WWL, the other station I had visited in Lafayette called to offer me a reporting position too, but I had already made up my mind.

Bill took a chance on me, and I will never forget how that affected my life and career. I always tell people that he is the man who discovered me. I realize now that people probably thought he was crazy to put a young girl with no TV experience on TV, but he believed in me. Sometimes, it takes just one person.

Preparation Is Key

I had a month to prepare for the traffic reporter position. The first goal was to try not to look superawkward on camera. Traffic reporters, like weathercasters, use a green screen, so the "map" that we are pointing to is actually a completely blank screen. We look at television screens on the side of the green screen to see what we are pointing to. So everything we refer to appears in the opposite position of where we see it, like a mirror image. Oh, and did I mention that I was the last person anyone would ever ask for directions? I couldn't give anyone directions to save my life, but I wasn't about to pass up a great opportunity because of that. I knew if I tried hard enough, I could learn to navigate the city just as I could learn anything else. Mike Hoss stepped in once again with some great advice. He told me to get in a car, drive around the city, and actually pay attention to how certain streets ran and options for getting from one major area of the city to another. It helped. I have lived in New Orleans my entire life, and while I could get anywhere, I couldn't explain to anyone how to get anywhere. I printed maps of the major roadways in our area and learned them like the back of my hand. Now, my family members do a double take when I have a better route somewhere than they do.

I practiced for weeks. I would do pretend traffic reports in front of the green screen for hours, tape them, and then have whoever was willing to watch give me feedback. My hand motions were awkward. I was speaking too quickly, and my voice was too high pitched. I could not gracefully move from one side of the green screen to the other. (The solution was to stay on one side. It took me months to move to the other side without being awkward.) But every day I got better.

I also spent a lot of time shadowing the traffic reporter who was leaving for a new job. She showed me the ropes and her workflow for the morning, which was very helpful. Typically, traffic reporters make beat calls to find out traffic information. At WWL, we have a company that supplies the traffic information. All I had to do was look at a computer screen that color-coded all of the accidents, construction projects, and any other road issues.

Doing More Than Expected

In May 2012, just a few months after I turned twenty-three, I worked my first day on air as a traffic reporter. Watching tape of that day now, I can see how much I've grown. My body language has become more natural, relaxed, and confident, which makes a huge difference.

Before I knew it, people who had worked at the station for decades were telling me that I was doing a really great job, and I was getting a traffic story on the evening news every now and then. I did a piece on a woman who had been given a speeding ticket in a school zone. The school zone hours had recently changed, but the city had never changed the signs on the street. So most drivers had no idea. There was always story material in the traffic department, from bridges breaking to events in town causing major detours. Our news managers have to fill hours' worth of shows a day. They are always hungry for content. Many of my stories were evergreen, which means they were not time sensitive and could have been used at any time. So I would finish my stories and wait. Within a week, the news managers would be light on news one day and thrilled to have my story. Once I had proven that I could do those stories, more opportunities popped up. Sometimes, I was put on a story simply because I was there. A reporter would call in sick, and I was able to fill in doing non-traffic-related stories.

I did not *have* to do anything after the morning show was over. After nine o'clock in the morning, no one really looked for me, except for the rare occasion of a major traffic incident before the noon show. But I knew that if I wanted to get ahead, I would have to do more than the bare minimum. Instead of wasting the second half of my shift playing on the computer, I worked on news stories. To me, this was being paid to train for my next job while being paid to do my current job.

My first day on air at WWL as a traffic reporter, May 30, 2012.
(Photograph by author)

There were many times when I could have slacked off, but it was up to me to use that time to better myself. Ultimately, I am the only person responsible for where I end up. The only person I would have shortchanged by doing less work was myself. My next move was always on my mind. If I wanted to be a traffic reporter for the rest of my life, I gladly would have left after the show ended. I had to want more for myself and expect more from myself than anyone else did.

The Nontraditional Route

My start on TV in my hometown and in a midsize market is a fairy tale to many who aspire to work in the business. I meet so many young girls who tell me they want to follow my footsteps exactly. But they are trying to follow my path from what they saw on TV, which isn't the whole story. I don't think that I ever would have gotten the traffic reporting job if I would have been focused on just trying to hurry up and get on TV. Some people assume I was just sitting around in the newsroom for a few months and was then magically picked to be the new on-air talent. Many young people have come to the station since and tried to follow in my footsteps, but they were following only the convenient ones.

When I left the traffic position, several people at the station—some who had never even shown interest in reporting—wanted me to help them prepare to apply for the spot. Of course, I did, but they were missing big chunks of how I got to where I was. I was not even thinking about working on air, specifically at WWL, when I was an associate producer. I was tirelessly working on my reporting skills because I was determined to get a reporting job, no matter where in the country I had to go. I had conversations with management about my goals and vision. I don't think that Bill would have ever thought about giving me that job if I had not had conversations with him about wanting to report and had not shown him through my résumé reels that I was improving. Some of the people who asked me to help them never worked on their reporting skills. They were just trying to jump on a convenient opportunity. On top of that, most of them had never even talked to Bill about being interested in the position, and he was the one who had to hire them. I didn't have any say in who would be hired next. I was glad that I had taken the time to ask questions and understand what steps I needed to take to get where I wanted to be.

I have found that when I do the work, opportunity follows. Lucky breaks are great—and I was very grateful for mine—but what's even greater is knowing I could have gotten exactly where I am without waiting for a lucky break. Taking shortcuts is a waste of time. I spent my time improving. It didn't go unnoticed.

My grandpa. (Photograph by author)

10

"Are You the News Lady?"

Look twice before you leap.

Charlotte Brontë

Being Recognized

It was an amazing and rare opportunity to get an on-air job in my hometown not long after graduating from college. I was grateful that my mom, dad, and grandpa could all be at home watching when I made my debut as WWL's traffic reporter in May 2012. My grandpa is always proud when one of his friends tells him they saw me on the news, but he also calls my mom when he thinks my skirts are too short. My dad is even more proud to scream, literally, to everyone that he is my father. A lawmaker whom I interview often told me that my dad flagged him down once on the street to introduce himself and let him know he was "Sheba's father." My mom texts me all the time to tell me that I am amazing.

Though I appreciated that they were able to watch me, I had a lot of growing to do, and I knew that I would inevitably make mistakes along the way. Many people go to small markets, have their embarrassing and awkward moments on air, and then move on to another market, where new viewers will never know anything of their past struggles. I would experience my growing pains in my hometown. Thankfully, the people of my city embraced me as if they all had a hand in raising me. On my first day on TV, a fellow Dominican High School graduate called to say that I had confused east and west, and that she liked me already so she wanted to help me out. It was weird to be out in public and suddenly have people recognize me. When I go to the grocery store, I hear, "Are you the news lady? We watch you every morning, and we love you." Viewers all feel as if they know me. I am so thankful that I can say ninety-nine percent of the feedback I get is positive.

I immediately started getting requests to emcee galas around the city, speak at graduations, and attend other community events. The best part of being a local celebrity was being invited to visit local schools and talk with students about my job. Since I was becoming a face that people recognized, I could help draw attention to important causes around the city. And I wanted to help as much as I could. I was celebrity judging, emceeing, and speaking as if it was my second job. I considered it part of my job to give back to the community and do positive things in the city.

I was also being interviewed for local magazines. They wanted me to share my story of growing up in New Orleans and working on TV in my hometown. I always have a good time at the photo shoots that accompany the interviews, and I love sharing more of my story with people in my community.

The Ugly Side of the Attention

Always Putting on a Show

In some ways, working in the news reminds me of performing in the theater. I love being part of a live show, where anything can happen. It keeps me on my

My feature in New Orleans Magazine, *2014.* (Photograph by Greg Miles)

toes and never gets dull. But being on TV is my least favorite part of my job. I did not get into this business for attention. If newspapers were not known as a dying business, I probably would have just become a writer. While I was very grateful for the support I received from the community, it didn't take long for me to feel burdened by always having to uphold the perfect persona I portrayed on the news. If I had a bad day, I couldn't come to work moping or giving off an angry vibe because I was on TV. There was no such thing as hiding in my cubicle and avoiding my coworkers until the day was over. The performance didn't end when the TV went off, because I might be recognized in the grocery store or gas station. I started feeling as if I never got to stop acting.

Constant Criticism

I instantly became a target of constant criticism. People think TV personalities have teams of people controlling our social media, doing our hair, and handling our emails. I visited a classroom to tell students about my job, and one girl asked if I had security with me when I went to the grocery store! People emailed that they didn't like how my makeup artist did my makeup that day. Too bad—I was the makeup artist. I noticed that the negative comments were overwhelmingly sent to women more than men, and most of the time, the comments had nothing to do with our work. I was

My natural hair after reporting in New Orleans humidity. (Photograph by author)

shocked that people called the news station or emailed to say they didn't like my hair or dress. One woman called the newsroom to complain about my hair being frizzy in 90° New Orleans heat, in which humidity was off the charts. Mostly, I brush off the comments, because I find that people who are quick to be critical of others have the most work to do on themselves.

A Social Life in the Public Eye

Being on TV affected my social life too. People whom I hadn't spoken to in years—and some I knew only from a distance—were suddenly interested in hanging out more. I am naturally very friendly, so it was difficult for me to be more guarded and question people's motives for wanting to be around me. There is this idea that with fame, life is easier and things are perfect because people know your name. I know this sounds crazy in a world where achieving social-media fame is a common goal and being famous for the sake of being famous is revered, but being recognized did not make me any happier.

Social Media

Social media certainly complicates having a personal life and a job where credibility is important. This was one of the few times I could not look to my coworkers for advice. Social media wasn't around when they were young and kicking off their careers. I used social media casually before I was on TV, but I never told everything about my life and whereabouts online. But social media still influenced my life. For my twenty-fourth birthday, I went out with some friends. I was having a good old time on the dance floor when I got an alert on my phone. It was a tweet. Someone in the club had recognized me and posted, saying that I was acting wild in the club. Talk about a damper on the fun. It was hard to let loose and enjoy the rest of the night. I felt as though my every move was being watched, judged, and documented, and sometimes it is.

Bring on the Crazy

Since this is the off-air version of my story, I want to reveal the attention TV personalities get that no one else sees. In my desk drawer, I keep a folder of crazy things people send me. The absolute worst offenders are the creepy men. Then there are the people who have made countless complaints about how I dress, how much makeup I wear, or how my hair is done. There are people who have turned my photo into their background photo on social

ibmitted a comment to Sheba Turk on www.wwltv.com:
-TV and WWLTV.com

r 14, 2012 10:55 AM

you look some good girl if you need a good man let me know somrthin

One of the many creepy emails I have received over the years. (Photograph by author)

---

an idea for you, Ms. Turk   Page 1 of 1

Reply   Reply All   Forward

an idea for you, Ms. Turk

Molly

To: Turk, Sheba

                                                    Friday, December 14, 2012 11:24 AM

i'm new to town and used to work professionally as a wrestler now i'm a coach, trainer of wrestlers and i've been trying to get some local celebrities and young professionals in the area together to step in the ring with me, i'll train you, you'll be body-slammed, suplexed, put in submission holds, but i'll be very gentle and safe with you, you won't be hurt, but yes you must be in great shape. i don't know how much you know about wrestling so you can look it up on YouTube or something if you like or ask me any questions you like. anyway for my clarification so i know how to handle you in the ring, how tall are you, how old are you and are you in good physical condition? as i said i'll be very careful with you and everyone else so if you're interested let me know i want to get this started asap. what do you say, Ms. Turk, do you have what it takes to step in the ring with me?

A creepy comment from a viewer. (Photograph by author)

media. I have gotten advertisements for bras in the mail, letters from prisoners, used perfume samples ripped out of magazines, flowers, jewelry, a sanitary napkin, and the list goes on. Once I think I've seen it all, I get something else.

Handling the Attention

Changing My Mind-Set

Just as I started being bothered by the attention, I attended one of Soledad's PowHERful enrichment conferences for young girls. The PowHERful conferences are free daylong events for high-school- and college-aged young women that focus on educational, professional, and personal development. At this conference, rapper MC Lyte told a story that I was meant to hear. In a bathroom stall when she was out one night, she overheard two women talking about her. She remembered wishing that no one knew who she was. Not long after, she felt as if her professional life took a dive. She warned attendees to be careful about what we think and speak into existence. After hearing her speak, I stopped wallowing in negative thoughts about the attention I was getting. If I wanted to be in this business and be successful, people would know my name, and wishing otherwise was hoping that I would fail. I was so grateful that I heard this cautionary tale early in my career. It changed my perspective on being in the public eye.

Thinking about My Brand

Even though I learned to accept my newfound attention, there were still some things I needed to tweak to make sure my real life was not a detriment to my professional goals. I am a brand. Everything I do adds or takes away from that brand. The events I chose to be involved with, the people I chose to be around, and my posts on social media were all a part of my brand. I had to ask myself if they painted a picture that reflected me and what I stood for.

When I post on social media, I think about how I want to be perceived and post pictures to build that image. I post about events I emcee, any positive accomplishments surrounding my career—promotions, awards, magazine features—and promotions for my show. The most feedback I get is on pictures that show me just hanging around the studio. People love the lighthearted posts that show my personality. I am also always careful to reflect the appropriate tone of the story I'm covering. A selfie with a puppy at a dog show is fun and fitting, but a selfie on a murder scene is completely inappropriate. It seems obvious, but I have seen people in the business make mistakes in this area.

I post often but not every second of my day. I keep most of my real life off social media. My closest friends, my boyfriend, and my family don't appear often on my page, because my relationships with them are personal and I don't want them subjected to the criticism I face. I also don't post pictures of me with alcohol, because they do nothing for my brand and could be taken out of context. One of my coworkers warned me that before being on TV, I should remove from online everything that I wouldn't want anyone else to see, and it was great advice. I would have never thought that people would dig up old pictures of me.

Credibility is huge for news anchors. Having it means that people can trust me as their news source. I can't expect to post wild pictures all night, roll into work in the morning, and have people not judge me. I always try to imagine what I would think about myself if I were looking from the outside. I don't believe in having private accounts where I could post things I wouldn't want viewers or my employer to see. The content would be easy to screenshot, and suddenly a picture is not private. It's just not worth my career or reputation.

Just Don't Respond

When I first started working on camera, I tried to respond to everyone— good and bad. Big mistake. Negative comments don't even deserve a response. I learned that I could always win by staying silent, but it took me a little while to learn to fight that initial urge to respond. Oddly, the few times I have responded to criticism, the person always backs down. Once, a man emailed the entire station that he didn't like me and was switching channels. I was annoyed at the email but even more annoyed that he sent it to all of my coworkers, including my boss. I replied by first correcting all of his grammatical mistakes and then telling him to email someone who cared. He responded that he didn't think on-air talent actually read their emails. He apologized and requested my autograph (which I did not send).

Sadly, responding to positive comments can backfire too. When I debuted on TV, I was so grateful that people were welcoming that I wanted to respond to everyone who contacted me. But some people emailed or tweeted at me so much I had to block them. A few men took my "thank you" as "yes, please keep emailing me about how I look and the imaginary future you have envisioned between us." I learned the hard way that in most cases, it's best not to respond at all.

Don't Take It to Heart

After a while, it got much easier to ignore people who commented that my clothes were too tight or revealing, because those are personal preferences. People who hide behind computers and phones and criticize others are pathetic anyway. But there were also rare comments on my actual work. I got an email early on in my traffic reporting days from a person clearly trying to be rude and demeaning. He said I spoke too quickly and that my voice was too high pitched. Both were issues I was working on. I don't remember responding, but I did look past his rudeness and use the comment to better myself.

Keys to Confidence

Focusing on Me

The criticism never stops, so I am very grateful that I came into this business as a very confident person. Young girls often ask me how I am able to be confident. I focus on myself and not others, which plays a huge role in being confident. When I focus on what other people are doing, it's easy to get distracted from all the great things about me. I also find that being critical of others makes me worry about what other people think of me even more. If I bad-mouth someone, it's only natural to assume people are bad-mouthing me.

People also love to make comparisons, especially among women on TV. Sometimes, people stop me to say they like someone on another channel. They assume we all know each other, since we all live in TV world. I always nod politely and carry on. Other times, they stop to tell me that they don't like someone else. I never take the bait. There is this perception that women are always at odds, and that only one of us can succeed at a time. We can all succeed. I don't have to bash other women to make myself look better. I like to throw people off guard. I often say, "Oh yeah, she's great." And if I don't have something nice to say, I don't say anything at all.

Everyone in the same industry is technically in competition with each other, but I don't like to think of life as a competition. I know that what is meant for me will be for me. There are enough amazing opportunities for everyone. I have not run into a situation yet where it is advantageous to focus on what people around me have going on. I am running my own race in life.

Staying True to Myself

When I stopped forcing myself to wear dress pants, I became a lot more confident. It wasn't about the clothes. It was about being me and being comfortable. I am always more confident when I am being true to myself, whether that's in the way I dress or what words I decide to use in a live report. Many times, the newsroom will get information from police or other city officials, and the language is very stuffy: "The male victim expired adjacent to the home." I wouldn't feel confident talking like someone else. I am more confident when I reword stories to sound like something I would actually say. I feel more relaxed and natural because those words are natural to me. I find it hard to be confident when I am doing something that is not genuine.

Always Trying My Best

A lot of my confidence also comes from knowing that I always put forth my best effort. I know that if events don't turn out the way I want them to, it's due to some force outside of me. Sometimes, there is a challenge in setting up a live shot. The traffic computer malfunctions, and I end up standing in front of a blank screen. The person I am supposed to interview doesn't show up. So many things can go wrong in the news world. I have to trust that I did all I could beforehand to make things run smoothly, and I have to trust that I'll take a deep breath and deal with everything that goes wrong as it comes.

When I'm Not Feeling Confident

Prep More

In an ideal world, we would all achieve a high level of confidence and never have to worry about it again. I feel good about myself most of the time, but I definitely have moments when I am not feeling very confident. I was not very confident at all when I first got the traffic reporter position, because I did not know anything about navigation. My lack of confidence was rooted in a lack of knowledge.

Imagine being on a stage, being asked to give the history of the ivory trade, and not knowing anything about it. You wouldn't be very confident. Now if this were something you had studied for years and could talk about for hours, you wouldn't be so nervous. Knowledge is a big confidence boost. When I know what I am talking about and I can own it, I am more confident. If I am not naturally good at something, I practice and learn more until I start to feel more confident. My co-anchors have been in the business for decades, so they can breeze through some interviews without any preparation. For those same interviews, sometimes I need to spend a considerable amount of time doing research. Things do get easier. The next time that topic comes up, I don't have to do as much work. The key is realizing that getting better isn't going to happen naturally. I had to watch myself, make notes, and work on making specific changes.

Accept the Awkward

There is nothing worse than watching someone struggle to do something while everyone else watches in amusement. When I make a mistake, I find the best way to avoid feeling as if everybody is talking about it is to call myself out first and make light of an otherwise tragic situation. Imagine trying to tape a stand-up and messing up several times in front of a crowd of people. Make a joke, like, "Third time's the charm." I acknowledge that it happened and keep it moving. Dwelling on my mistakes only makes me feel less confident on my next attempt.

Fake It

When all else fails, I just pretend to be confident. This is one of the rare times I am going to encourage faking it. Of course, I did not feel confident when I first jumped in front of a camera, but I stood up tall and tried my best to look as if I knew what I was doing.

People are often shocked to find out that I didn't always feel confident emceeing events. I love speaking to an audience, but I feel as though emceeing comes with a pressure to be entertaining. I forced myself to practice my delivery and feel more comfortable, and as time has passed, I have started to feel better about my skills.

When I am not feeling confident, it also helps me to imagine the worst that could possibly happen. I could mess up, make a fool out of myself, get embarrassed—basically, in some form or another, fail—but not doing whatever I'm not confident about is also failing. When I think about it like that, I don't have anything to lose.

11

Set Yourself up for More Opportunity: Be Present, Be Productive, and Be Positive

Working hard and working smart sometimes can be two different things.

Byron Dorgan

Be Present

I really enjoyed being a traffic reporter, but I took the position knowing that I wanted more. Being part of the morning show was lots of fun. I was getting opportunities to report, and since we gave traffic updates nearly every ten minutes, I was getting plenty of exposure. I started filling in more often when other reporters were out, even though I still wasn't completely comfortable with it. I was always doubting whether I knew enough or was asking the right questions as I conducted interviews for my stories. There is a formula when it comes to putting together a news story that I hadn't mastered yet. A typical news story is a minute and thirty seconds. I struggled to write a story under three minutes. I spent more time cutting things out of the story than actually writing it. There is also a particular way the story needs to be formatted in the computer system so that it looks right on air, and sometimes I was still getting it wrong. Soledad and Kim told me that half the battle of being successful was just showing up and doing my job well every day. I didn't have any real strategy for becoming a reporter besides showing up and doing my best.

That meant working longer than eight hours when I was trying to finish a story or fill in for a reporter. I got my big break when Hurricane Isaac hit. The opportunity didn't come my way because I was the best. I was just there, and I stepped up. Hurricane Isaac hit New Orleans in August 2012. I had been on TV since May, so I didn't have much experience. I always knew that going into news meant not evacuating in the event of a storm. There are a lot of things about this business that are counterintuitive to normal human instincts. We run toward crime scenes, not away from them. When it's storming, we

115

head outside to check it out instead of ducking for cover. And when there is a chemical plant fire with the possibility of dangerous fumes in the air, we jump in the car and drive toward it. Part of being a reporter is knowing that I'll be left behind as my family evacuates for a storm and that I'll be standing right next to police officers searching for an armed suspect.

I was fine with staying for a hurricane and doing all those other things that feel unnatural. I believe that when it's our time to die, it's our time, which keeps me from being afraid in dangerous situations. I am always sensible, because no story is worth risking my life for. When the storm came, though, it did feel weird, and the reality hit that my parents would be evacuating without me. My mom wanted to stay, but I told her that I would be safe at the station and I would work better knowing they were safe in Texas with family.

The day before the storm hit, New Orleanians started evacuating, and traffic was a mess. Technically, my traffic contract did not require that I stay during an evacuation, since I wasn't a WWL employee. The traffic reporter position is contracted through a company that WWL pays to supply the station with traffic information. But it didn't even occur to me to leave. I stayed on air doing traffic hits all day. I had come to work at four in the morning, and at about six or seven in the evening, my boss said I should go home and sleep but pack clothes, because when I came back I wouldn't be leaving again until the storm was over. WWL has a lot of employees. We are usually split up over shifts, so all employees aren't in the building at one time on a regular day. During storms, everyone stays at the station. We have long shifts, finding a few hours to sleep at a spot around our desks or on an old office floor when we get to take a break.

The next day, I stayed on TV, keeping up with traffic all day, but when the storm finally hit, I felt useless. We carried twenty-four-hour coverage, so the station needed to fill time. I didn't see the point in doing traffic when no one was driving. I went into Bill's office and told him that I could be more helpful if I went to check out some of the areas our reporters hadn't made it to yet, such as Gentilly, where I lived. He said that he didn't have any more photographers available. I knew that one of our studio cameramen wanted to be a field photographer, so I suggested that I use him. It was the perfect situation. The newsroom is always desperate for content, my news director had faith in me, so he said yes. So there we were, the wannabe photographer and the wannabe field reporter headed for Gentilly. It was raining but not that hard. There were lots of trees and some power lines down in the street. We went straight to the gas station at Elysian Fields Avenue and I-610, where a sign had been knocked over by the wind and cracked. I taped several pieces that I laugh at now—because they still weren't very good. I came back with content, and it was good enough, apparently, for storm coverage. The photographers edited a few of the pieces, and I tried to make myself look decent to head to the set. Appearance plays a huge factor in anything that is visual, such as TV, but during a storm, we are often scrambling, sweating, rain soaked, flustered, and too focused on our stories to think about how we look.

When I came from shooting in the storm, my hair was soaking wet. And I have huge kinky curly hair. I slicked it down with handfuls of gel and threw it into a bun. I sat with Angela Hill and Dennis Woltering, two legendary anchors at our station, and talked with them on air about everything I had seen on the street and what I was hearing from people about their biggest concerns. My boss and some other higher-ups in the company were impressed. Not long after the storm was over, the news director called me into his office to compliment me on my work during the storm. Bill said that if a reporter position opened, he would strongly consider giving it to me. When Isaac hit the city, I could have stayed in the warm, dry studio, but going out in that storm put me one step closer to my ultimate goal.

Months after the storm, I kept doing traffic stories and filling in for other reporters. I could have been off for Christmas, because there were no traffic reports. The station needed someone to do the morning show reporting shift, so I volunteered. Our morning show executive producer, Val Amedee, who has also been very supportive of my growth, helped me pull some ideas together, and there I was Christmas morning 2012, doing live shots on a possible shutdown of the federal government. I must admit, the story was very intimidating. I wasn't anything close to a government or financial expert. I had kept up with news of the looming shutdown, but that was it. Prior to my shift, I stayed up late reading everything I could about the issue. Our anchors—Sally Ann Roberts, Eric Paulsen, and Mike Hoss—gave me tips on what to focus on. I had underestimated myself. I did just fine. I didn't feel secure during my first live shot, but by the end of the morning, I felt relieved. I had survived a shift as a morning show reporter. And like every next step I took, it wasn't so scary on the other side.

In February, the Super Bowl came to town. I was asked to be part of an entertainment special that would air live each night during the week leading up to the Super Bowl. I still had to report traffic at five in the morning, which meant my day wouldn't end until almost ten o'clock at night. I could have complained about my hours or about having to work two jobs, but I knew this was a great opportunity. It was a long week, but a rewarding one. Dominic Massa was producing the live show, and everything turns out okay when he has a hand in it. He was superhelpful, as he always is. And there were some cool opportunities that week that kept me engaged even though I was working nonstop. I was sent to a Super Bowl press conference where Beyonce was speaking, since she was the halftime performer for the game. It was right after the scandal where she admitted to lip-synching the national anthem at President Barack Obama's inauguration ceremony for his second term in office. She started the press conference by singing the national anthem live to prove that she could sing the song without any vocal assistance. Hello—free mini Beyonce concert anyone? Later that night, I got to recap what happened at the press conference for the live show. At the station, I took on a lead role for a project, and once again, Bill was happy with my work.

Being present is certainly not about being perfect. I am often asked if we ever mess up on TV. I don't think people ever stop making mistakes. The important thing is to learn from them. Unfortunately, the effect of making mistakes on TV will be amplified by the fact that others will see them.

One of my most memorable mistakes happened when I was reporting traffic. I had to remember when to pause for commercial breaks. Well, one time I tossed to a commercial break that wasn't there, and so I just stood staring into the screen for an awkward amount of time until the director told me in my ear that I did not have a break. I was mortified. I confessed to viewers that there was no break and finished my report. I couldn't get off TV fast enough. I don't think anyone remembers that moment except me.

Be Productive toward *My* Goals

The more I made myself available, the more opportunities came my way. Being present was step one. Step two was making sure I was getting something out of being there. As an intern, I was always willing to be helpful, but I had to make sure I was getting something out of the work. Maintaining that balance is key to advancing in the workplace.

One of the most important things I have learned is that hard work is not enough. The hardest working people in a newsroom are not necessarily the highest paid or the most valued. I find the highest paid and most valued are the people who know their worth, speak up for themselves, and are strategic about benefiting from their work. I also started to notice this was true in all areas of life. The most famous singers are not necessarily the best singers. There is more to it than just being good or working hard, and I think the key is being strategic. It's truly quality not quantity when it comes to the time you put in at work.

I wanted to be helpful to the station, but I also needed to be helpful to myself. I needed to be present in moments and on tasks that would help me grow and learn. That balance will not always be possible. There are times that I am asked to do a ton of things that don't really benefit me, and that is fine because there are other experiences that allow for self-advancement and growth. Being productive isn't just about getting work done for the company. It's about finding a way to do that work that puts me closer to the big picture. It's always about the big picture.

Be Positive

I was the first person in Soledad's PowHERful Foundation to graduate from college. The foundation pays for young girls to attend college and provides everything that a young lady might need to finish college, including mentoring. Four years after I graduated, Soledad invited me to be the keynote speaker for her PowHERful summit in New Orleans, which meant speaking to a crowd of young girls about my journey and the lessons I had learned along the way.

Soledad spoke to the young girls after me and started to explain why she decided to give me the money I needed to finish college. She explained that she meets many girls who ask for her help, but she really invests in the ones who are what she called "sure bets." These are young ladies who are just one small step away from accomplishing their goals, but one obstacle is standing in their way. For me, that was the money I needed to graduate. Soledad had endless requests from young girls about mentoring and career advice, so I had always wondered why she had used her time and resources to help me. She told the audience that despite all of my obstacles, I was always positive. I remembered that one day, she had asked me why I was always so positive, and I had to search for an answer. I had never really given it much thought.

Being positive isn't something I do purposefully. This is just my natural disposition. But there have been rare times when my first reaction was not to be positive. In those moments, I can imagine what it's like for people whose natural disposition is different from mine. For me, it's pretty simple. I want to be happy, confident, calm, and in control of me. If I let what someone says or something that happens change that, I see it as a weakness on my part. I don't let circumstances change me, because I want to be more than a reaction. I strive to be the same person I decide to be every day. Who I am on a particular day does not depend on if one of my coworkers is upset and has an attitude, or if a driver decides to cut me off. Of course, we might want to scream at the person or get angry, but then I feel I have lost. I allowed this person who has no significance in my life to decide that I am going to be angry. It gives me peace of mind to know that no one else has power over my emotions. Thinking about moving forward actually helps me not waste time dwelling on the past or negative options. I am drawn to people who are positive, uplifting, and always looking for solutions, so I strive to be that myself.

How to Be Positive

Thinking about the People Who Have Sacrificed for Me

When everything is going right, it is easy to be positive, but of course, things won't always go as I want them to. In her speech at the summit, Soledad pointed out that I could have been angry when I had to leave NYU or I could have decided not to finish college. The truth is that quitting never crossed my mind, and that's in my genes. At almost sixty years old, my mom is still working on her undergraduate degree in psychology. She started college right after high school, dropped out, and went back several times. My parents sacrificed so much of their lives to put me through school and make sure that I had great opportunities that I couldn't even imagine telling them I was giving up.

Persevering through a Tough Time

I like to think I am a practical person. I am not one to waste much time on dramatic reactions to a situation, which really are not helpful. When things are not going my way, I weigh my options. After leaving NYU, I could have decided to quit college, but I had a vision for my life and career that involved going to college. Hard times are the best times to focus on my goals. My mom has always told me to use tunnel vision. Things will be dark, but just keep moving toward the light at the end of the tunnel.

My ability to be so positive also comes from my faith. I believe there is a higher power looking out for me and that things play out the way they do for a reason. We can't see the big picture, so one bad moment makes us feel as if everything is crashing down. I had to learn to be patient. I was miserable just sitting around my home, broke, after I left NYU, but when I look at how great things are going for me now, I realize I wasted time worrying and being frustrated about not being in school. Since then, anytime things look bad, I think of how things have turned out and keep it moving. I have accepted that the rough times are just as much a part of the plan as the good times. I don't want to diminish the fact that people go through some really tough and terrible times—illnesses, heartbreaks, financial hardships—but learning to be positive when things aren't good helps me get through the tough times.

Realizing You Can't Go Any Lower

I was not afraid of taking risks because I didn't have anything to lose. If I failed and didn't make it as a reporter, I would be exactly where I started. So why not try? I was never afraid to hit rock bottom, because I was already there. I could only go up. I was not hesitant to leave a good thing for something better. It took me almost quitting at WWL to get promoted.

My carefree attitude helped me brush off a lot of small things that could have distracted me. It's easy to get wrapped up in what other people have going on and start comparing myself to others. I had to remember that I was running my own race. It didn't matter what anyone else was doing, because it didn't really affect the things I was working on for myself. When everyone else was panicking, I liked to remain calm.

I didn't have a carefree life growing up—actually, just the opposite. My parents struggled financially, so there was always something I could have spent time worrying about. There was so much going on that most things seemed trivial. If I had a bad day at school, I brushed it off, thinking at least it was over and tomorrow would be better. And not being able to afford some things really wasn't the worst thing ever. At the end of the day, I had what I needed: my family and my future. The struggle made me stronger. Throughout the years, several of my friends have passed comments pointing out that nothing seems to bother me. That is not true, but it does take a lot to upset me. I learned that I could be in control of my life by controlling my reactions to everything going on around me. I could have turned out to be an adult who is paranoid about having money problems and ended up chasing a check. Instead, I thought if I made it all these years without money, I could do it a little bit longer to pursue my dreams.

I stayed in that mind-set even after I started earning decent money. I kept living as if I was not making much money. I didn't buy a new car. I drove my 2004 Toyota Corolla, which I had bought from a coworker for $3,000 after college. In fact, I kept driving it through my first three-year contract as an anchor. It had battle wounds—dents, scratches—from a few accidents. The hubcaps popped off, but I still kept it moving. Yes, I could have easily gotten some hubcaps to give my little Corolla, who I called Butter, a little pop. But I really couldn't have cared less what that car looked like. I wanted to be out of student loan debt. I lived at home with my parents and sent most of my paycheck to Sallie Mae, Fed Loan, and that other terrible private loan company. My parents taught me that sacrifice was worth it to achieve my long-term goals. I couldn't see it then, but many of the financial struggles that I once thought of as disadvantages made me stronger and gave me a unique perspective. I looked at money and material things very differently than the people I was surrounded by.

Being a Person I Would Want to Be Around

I do not like to be around people who are always complaining or whining about their problems. It's frustrating to hear someone complaining about a problem that is trivial compared with other people's problems. I am not saying that we should all keep everything to ourselves. I talk to my family and friends about my problems all the time.

Everyone is going through something, and many of us are going through the same things: financial issues, family problems, uncertainty about our professional paths. It is how we react to those issues that sets us apart. Kim and Soledad told me that being positive drew them to me, because they knew that I was struggling to finish college. I could not believe that all of these amazing opportunities had come to me mainly because of my attitude.

Kim laid it out plain and simple for me one day. People want to work with people they like. If I were in a position to hire someone and both candidates had similar backgrounds, would I would hire the one I liked more? The answer is yes. I have never strived to be liked, but I was always being told by my mentors that being liked was a good thing. I kept brushing it off. My mom had always taught me that life was not a popularity contest, so I don't waste time wondering if people like me or not. But when Bill decided to put me on air, he echoed Kim and Soledad, saying that it was great that people just seemed to like me.

Being liked can be a marketable skill, and I say skill because a person can work on being more likable. I have been told that people like that I come off as honest and real. Fake may sell on reality TV, but no one likes someone who is phony or trying to prove themselves. It comes off as insecure. I put all my truths out there, and if people like me, they like me. If they don't, it really doesn't matter. Throughout my career, being nice and friendly certainly did not work against me, but I did have to learn to balance being laid-back with making sure people took me seriously when it was time to do business.

A good attitude can come in handy when I have issues with scripts written for me by producers. The facts may be wrong, a major part of the story could be missing, or there are typos. I may not like the order of stories in a show. Maybe there is a funny story followed by a report of a murder. Segments need to flow effortlessly. In these instances, I had to learn to speak up, because viewers see only me. So they will blame me for all of those mistakes. Some anchors yell and scold producers, and sadly, sometimes producers treat the people who yell at them better than those who don't. There is a difference between respect and fear. I don't want people to be afraid of me, but I find people respect me when I hold them accountable for their actions. We all make mistakes, but I couldn't keep brushing things that weren't working under the rug because I wanted to be nice. Being liked is great, but being respected is more important.

12

Being a Reporter

The harder I work, the luckier I get.

Unknown

Signing a Contract

I had been a traffic reporter for less than a year, when a position opened for a general assignment reporter. As Bill had promised, he threw me in the running for the position. Not long after the person who had the job left, Bill told me I got the promotion.

In college, I was working on a paper about the coverage of Latinos in the media, and I called Maya Rodriguez, after doing some research and finding that she was the only Spanish-speaking reporter at WWL at the time. I talked with her about her job as a general assignment reporter. Coincidentally, the general assignment job I was filling was her spot. She had decided not to renew her contract with the station. Just two years prior, I was asking her for help with homework. Now, I would be moving into her position.

This was huge. I was getting the job I wanted, at the station I wanted, and I would sign my first contract with a news station. I was not completely confident in my reporting abilities, but I had volunteered in the position enough to know that I could be as good as I wanted to be if I just kept working at it.

The contract would bring me into the fold of WWL staff. Traffic reporters sometimes have different setups from other employees. As I mentioned earlier, our traffic reporter technically works for another company that supplies traffic information, even though WWL still chooses that reporter. As a traffic reporter, I didn't even have the same payday as WWL employees. As a field reporter, I would officially be a full-time, on-air WWL employee.

Always Negotiate

Even though I barely had any experience as a field reporter, Kim told me that it was important to work on my negotiating skills. I would have to sit down and discuss my contract with Bill. Of course, money is usually the main negotiating point, but there are other elements that are often negotiable: the length of the contract, inclusion of what is called a non-compete clause (which is explained below), hair and makeup allowance, vacation, among other components.

A reporter's salary depends on the market. Twenty-four thousand dollars was the starting salary for a reporter in Lafayette, but the higher the market—the more viewers, the more money generated by a station—the more employees tend to earn. That's why the traffic position in New Orleans paid more than a higher position in a lower market in Lafayette. Some anchors (the highest position for on-air talent) in a small market make less money than a reporter in a larger market. I won't talk about my specific salary, because doing so violates my contract. Also, it won't really help anyone to know how much I make, since different variables, such as market size and experience, influence salary. Salary negotiation is one of the areas where my mentors were the most helpful. I trusted them enough to share all of the details of my contract, including salary, and they had enough knowledge to let me know if it was fair. My contract was pretty standard for a first-time reporting job in that market, but again, Kim insisted I negotiate. She said that it would show the station that I wouldn't be happy with just anything.

On-air talent signs what is called a personal services contract. By signing it, I would agree to work for the company for a certain number of years. In this case, it was three years with no "outs," so even if a New York station wanted to hire me, I was legally bound to WWL and would not be able to take the job. In other words, there was no way out until the contract ended.

I wanted a contract to work for two years at WWL as a field reporter. In two years, I would have a decent amount of experience and could negotiate for more pay. I was confident that after two years of reporting, I would have a shot at an anchor job or a better-paying reporting job, even if it meant I had to move away from New Orleans. I told Bill that I wanted to be an anchor in two years, so I did not want to sign a contract for three years as a reporter. Ignorance is bliss. I had never anchored a show in my life, but Bill agreed and gave me the two-year contract. My mentor was right. Negotiating did make me feel more confident that I could address issues that were important to me, and it made me feel as if I had a say in the direction of my career. I had also asked for a clothing and hair allowance. Some stations give on-air talent a certain amount to spend on their wardrobes. WWL did at one time, but Bill said the station no longer provided such an allowance.

Contracts for on-air talent also include a non-compete clause. This clause outlines a certain amount of time during which you cannot work at a competing station if you leave the company. This component was not a big deal to me. I felt good about the opportunities I had at WWL.

Working without an Agent

Some TV personalities pay a percentage of their salary to an agent to find jobs and negotiate for them. In my case, I found the job on my own, so I didn't need to pay someone a percentage of my salary, when the biggest hurdle was already over. The downside to not having an agent was that I needed to negotiate for myself. If I had hired an agent, I never would have spoken to my managers directly about my contract. I would have had professional negotiators speaking on my behalf—a definite benefit! But my mentors insisted that I didn't have much negotiating power anyway, since I hardly had any experience. They didn't think any agent could get me much more money than I had been offered. So I did everything myself. It was just the beginning of my journey, and I knew that next time, I would have more experience under my belt, which would give me more negotiating power.

Trial by Fire

"There's a shooting . . . on the Westbank . . . sounds like a woman and a few children. You need to go. Now."

Reporting in the field. (Photograph by Ricknise Riggins)

That was my first breaking news assignment as a reporter. It was four o'clock in the morning, and our morning show executive producer, Val Amedee, was calm as she always is but speaking with more urgency than I had ever experienced since I started at the station. I was anxious and not sure what to expect, but I grabbed my things and headed out of the door with my photographer, Willie Wilson. He's a veteran and legend in this business and retired in 2015. On this shoot, he was as cool as a cucumber. I was scared, but thankfully, I didn't really have time to think about how I felt.

Fifteen minutes later, we were at an apartment complex. There were men without shirts on, women with rollers in their hair, kids with pajama pants on—clear reminders that it was not even dawn. Investigators rolled out yellow crime scene tape. I got a call from my executive producer: "We need you to do a phoner [phone interview] in ten minutes."

I didn't know anything yet about what had happened, but I told her that I would be ready. I asked a deputy sheriff for details. He told me that I had to call the public information officer. I did, but there was no answer. I walked up to group of people who seemed afraid as I approached and asked them what they knew. I tried talking to as many people as I could, and I started getting fragments of information. Some helped me make more sense of things; others confused me even more.

A few minutes after arriving at the scene, I was live on the phone, giving my first report. I had heard that two women and several toddlers had been shot. I didn't know the victims' conditions, but I was hearing from neighbors that the woman who lived in the apartment where the shooting happened babysat for a lot of people in the neighborhood. Eventually, we learned that two women and three toddlers were shot and taken to the hospital.

I had prayed for one thing the night before: a quiet first day. That was one of the many times God completely ignored me and gave me exactly what I needed. The intensity of that day was a blessing in disguise, because I've never felt that fear again in the news business. I figured if I could handle that, I was ready for anything. When I got home that evening, I knew that all of my hard work the years before had finally paid off.

Reporting Live

Handling Emotion

From my first day, I learned a lot of lessons that I apply to every story I cover. At the scene, I started to talk about how sad it was that those babies were shot. Willie let me go on for a while and then stopped me. He asked me how I was going to tell people what was going on if I couldn't keep my composure. He told me to stay focused, and he was right. I am often asked if the stories we cover ever get to me. Of course, some do. I am particularly sensitive to stories about children and, even more so, young girls. I am so grateful for having extremely loving parents. I can't imagine how hard life is for children who don't have someone in their lives who really cares about them and protects them. There are times when I want to be angry or emotional, just as everyone else is about a story, but I can't get people the information they need if I am crying about what's going on. It's my job to separate myself from the story in order to deliver the story to viewers effectively.

Another story that was hard to cover was the murder of Ahlittia North, a little girl who was killed by a relative. Her step-cousin admitted he had sex with her and had stabbed her to death before throwing her in a trash can in front of her mother's apartment. I was there the morning her body was found. She was six. Only six. I still think about that story. Later reports found that she had been moved around a lot among family members. I imagine what her life was like before she was killed and all that she went through in that short life. I also think about the twenty-year-old step-cousin who clearly had some issues of his own. He was also extremely young and claimed that he was seduced by the six-year-old. I wondered if there were signs of his instability before Ahlittia's murder.

But there is more news and violence every day, so I moved on to the next story. In TV, we don't typically get days to follow up or dig into the same story unless it's a big one. Newspapers have more time to gather information and keep adding to stories.

The Ahlittia North case made a lot of New Orleanians angry, so there were people at the scene who wanted to talk. One man said her body had been found chopped up. We aired the interview with his comment about the body, but I did say that police were not able to confirm that information. Officials eventually emailed to say that was not true. I did address the misinformation on air, so that viewers were clear that the eyewitness account was not factual. Even when there is not a lot of information to pass along, I can't just repeat anything I hear, because it might not be true. It's better not to give out a lot of information than have to apologize for giving out information that turns out to be wrong. I always feel pressured to be first and move fast in the news business, but those tensions will never trump my commitment to providing factual information.

When I think about the stories that have made me the most emotional, I remember arriving on the scene of a deadly crash between a bus carrying students from Florida to New Orleans on a field trip and another car on the interstate out in New Orleans East in May of 2013. Crews brought in the Jaws of Life to remove the victim from the other car. I will never forget the feeling in my stomach when I realized there was a baby seat in the back of the mangled vehicle. We wouldn't learn until later that the baby was not in the car, but the young woman who was killed was a new mother.

Covering Breaking News

It was April 2013 when I survived my first official day on air as a general assignment reporter for WWL's morning show. I had spent my internship shadowing the general assignment reporter for the morning show at another station. Our morning show aired live from five to nine o'clock in the morning. We did not have a four thirty show then. I gave live reports nearly every half hour, and on a typical day, I covered two different stories, one for the early hours and something more lighthearted at eight o'clock. If there was breaking news, I might cover more or less. I prefer covering breaking news. I would never wish for something bad to happen, but it's in those moments, when people are really frustrated or panicking, that I feel the newsroom can really help by providing vital information. Aspiring journalists will often ask me about the

French Quarter, shooting a piece for WWL-TV. (Photograph by Ricknise Riggins)

difficulty of reporting breaking news, but I find it the easiest to cover. It happens instantly, so usually there isn't time to write out a full script. There is always an adrenaline rush, because things are happening so quickly, and I am trying to juggle a million tasks, such as getting information from witnesses, looking for officials on the scene, and communicating with the producers back at the station about what they need from me. And somewhere in there, I have to figure out something coherent to say. I just relay the information to the viewers step by step as it unfolds. I always think about what information I would want to know if I were sitting at home watching a story on the news.

With breaking news, I am not completely on my own out there on the scene. Producers are in my ear communicating information. Our executive producers are also back at the station making calls for extra information and keeping an eye out for emails from officials or eyewitnesses about the story. As the face of what happens while the station is live on the scene, I certainly have to take the lead. I communicate if I find someone to interview on TV. I give the producer a heads-up that a press conference may happen soon and that we will need to take it live.

There are many times when I have to go live and all I know is one fact—for example, that a murder took place. I still am obligated to talk for a certain amount of time in a show. The trick is to focus on what I do know and what is going on around me. Are police still on the scene? Is anyone else at the scene? Have I seen a coroner's van? Is the crime scene a home, car, or apartment building? The key is being observant and telling viewers what I see.

Reporter Workflow

As our morning show reporter, I got into the newsroom every day at around three thirty in the morning. My first live report on TV was usually at five. I liked going in early so that I had some extra time to work on scripts. I like to do as much research as I can ahead of time for stories that we plan to cover (not breaking news). When I get in, I usually do research, write a script, and sometimes create graphics to accompany my story. Early in my tenure at WWL, I found that I always needed more backstory to feel comfortable delivering material. The internet has been my best friend. I could just give a live report based on a press release, but many times, that's not where the real story is. For instance, a press release will say that a new jail is opening. That is the news, but I'd really be missing the story if I didn't mention the delays and problems surrounding the jail opening.

When I first started, I was intimidated if I wasn't familiar with a story. Then, I realized that as long as I had a few minutes, I could do some research and give the story more context. Many times, I reported on stories I had little or no knowledge of prior to being assigned to them, and that really did not put me at a disadvantage compared to other reporters, because I always did my research. I asked questions, made phone calls, and searched online.

The thing that makes live reporting difficult is that after all of that researching, my story can change in a heartbeat. I am often pulled from the story I am covering to one that I don't know anything about. Several times, I have arrived at the scene and received conflicting information. My solution is to remain straightforward and conversational. If witnesses are telling me different things, I make that part of the story and report that I am getting conflicting information and waiting to get some facts confirmed.

As a morning show reporter, I struggled with the same challenge as the WDSU reporter I shadowed. I was stuck at work twelve hours or more many days. At around nine o'clock, the managers gave assignments for the day, and often times, they would give me an assignment similar to someone who had just come in at nine o'clock. That person was bright eyed and bushy tailed, just starting their day, and could work on the story for hours and still be within their eight-hour shift. I had been up since before three o'clock in the morning, and I knew that it would take longer than the rest of my eight-hour shift to get most stories done. I was often worn out by the time I had a chance to go out and interview people for the story. Then, I still had to come back to the station to write it. It wasn't uncommon to just be starting to write a story at one or two in the afternoon. With all that being said, I never minded helping with a story for the evening news or taping something that could air later. The managers weren't doing it to be spiteful. They just needed help throughout the day and weren't really noticing that it would take a big portion of the day to work on something for the evenings. By three o'clock in the afternoon (almost twelve hours after I came in), I was often still scrambling to finish my work for the day. I was being paid overtime, and I needed the experience. So I never said anything. I just put my head down and worked.

Social Media

Social media is a huge part of my job. When I get to the scene of breaking news, I hustle to gather information and set up my first live shot. Then I go back to getting more information so that I am ready for my next live shot.

Often, if I have not posted on social media, I will get a text from the station asking me to tweet something so that the station can share it with our social media followers. The benefit of social media is that we can get information out at any time. We don't have to wait until we are live on TV to give updates. I try to share a picture, short video, or fact about the situation, and then I continue gathering information. Sometimes, I even tweet on the way to the scene, so people already know to look for updates.

Interviewing

Research Is Key

Reporters must be great at interviewing. The key to a good interview is making it feel like a natural conversation while still getting information. As with live reports, research is the key to a good interview. I always read articles on the person I am interviewing, check to see if I can find any other interviews that person has done, and read anything I can find on them. Then I make shorthand bullet points or ideas for questions. The goal is to get a real understanding of the topic or person. If I am confused about something, I'll ask someone else if they are confused by it too. I have found that if I can't find any clarity on the issue being discussed in the interview, that's probably a great question for my guest. Sometimes, the most obvious questions are best. I like to keep things simple with "Why?" "How will that work?" and "How did that go?" I don't like two-part questions. Interviewees don't have time to process two-part questions, so usually they answer just one or get confused. If I have a follow-up question, I ask it after I've gotten an answer to the initial one.

The amount of research depends on the type of interview. If it's a fashion or beauty segment or one highlighting an event, sometimes, preparation is as simple as knowing what topics will be covered in the interview or reading the press release for the event. These types of interviews are common for morning news shows.

There usually isn't time to do research for breaking news stories, but again, breaking news is about letting viewers know what's happening now. So my first questions always concern the who, what, when, where, and why. As the story develops, the history and background may become more relevant. And that's where being well read and connected to the news comes in. With that background, I have information that can add more depth and perspective to my understanding of a situation.

Listen

When I first started interviewing, I made the common mistake of trying to strictly follow my list of questions. I am not naturally a good listener. I am a very visual person, so if I hear something and do not see it in writing, the information may go in one ear and out the other. Remember, I was just an intern when I started interviewing. I wasn't confident in my skills, I was trying to prove myself, and I wanted to seem composed. I would be so focused on asking my next question that I was barely listening to what the person I interviewed was saying. That is just wrong. I realized it was best to come up with a list of talking points, pick a first question, and ask subsequent questions based on the interviewee's answers.

Politicians are as practiced as reporters are, so interviewing them can be difficult. I initially felt as if they were sort of answering my questions but always taking things in a positive direction that worked in their favor. With politicians, I find the key to interviewing them is to keep the question as simple as possible and keep them on track. There should be a lot of "but" and "how" follow-up questions: "That's great [or true], but . . ." And if they don't answer the question, I try asking several times. As a last resort, Kim suggests acknowledging that they have not answered the question and moving on.

Balancing the Interviewee's Desires with the Reporter's

Politicians aren't the only ones with their own agendas. Sometimes, the only reason someone will make themselves available for interviews is because they have something going on and they want to get the word out, make an announcement, promote an event, or push their latest cause. In the interview, I will touch on what they are there to discuss, and I'll bring up other relevant issues. I always like to be open and give people a heads-up about what I plan to ask them about. Many interviewees' public relations representatives will ask for questions, which journalists don't provide. I will give them a sense of what I plan to cover and, if they request them, some possible talking points. If they insist on talking points, sometimes, I have them send over some topics that would be relevant to discuss in the interview.

Live versus Taped Interviews

Sometimes, I do interviews live. Other times, they are taped so that I can have my photographer edit a piece of it (for a sound bite) to use later. I prefer live, because once it's done, it's done. But interviewing live does leave room for things to go wrong. The person I am interviewing could be nervous or give me one-word answers. Unless I have interviewed them before, I can never anticipate how much or how little someone will speak, and my producer decides how much time I have to fill in a show. The producers give time cues in my ear as the interview is going on so that I stay on time (definitely something to get used to).

When I review taped interviews for a sound bite, I'm looking for about fifteen seconds showing a coherent thought. This was hard for me to do at first, because I wasn't listening during the interview. I was just focusing on my questions and nodding as the person spoke. Now, I know a sound bite when I hear it, and I just need to go back and find exactly where the person said it.

The Trouble with Yes or No Questions

I may ask a yes or no question to get information, but typically, I ask those before or after the actual interview, because they are too short to be sound bites. Many times, I ask these questions off camera so that I can use my camera time to make the interviewee talk, not just give one-word answers.

Make Them Feel Comfortable

Making people feel comfortable is another skill I have worked on over the years. "The media" has gotten this negative image as the other, a voice that doesn't really understand what's happening, a voice that has an agenda. So I get that some people are afraid to have anything to do with reporters. Getting interviews with people can be difficult and frustrating, especially when I'm in a time crunch. I have been at murder scenes where people run from me when I walk up to them with a microphone in my hand. Sometimes, there is a person who wants to tell me everything that happened, but when I ask them to tell me their story on camera, they refuse. And I can understand their fears. They may fear being misunderstood or misinterpreted. They may not think they can articulate their point well enough. Some are concerned for their safety.

People come first. I always ask if someone wants to speak. If they say yes, I talk to them about mindless things while we set up. That way, by the time my photographer has the equipment set up and is ready to begin the interview, the guest is warmed up.

If they don't want to speak, I tell them I am not there to bother them. If no one feels comfortable talking, that could be part of the story. It might tell me something about the neighborhood and how people view authority. Sometimes, all I have to do is assure people that they can tell their story best. If I sense that someone is uneasy as I approach, I try talking to them first. I just have a conversation and then help move them through the same thing on camera. I try to put myself in their shoes. I'll say something like, "This must be scary to have this happen in your neighborhood," to get them talking, and then I ask them to be on camera. I never want to be seen as an "other." I am just another member of the community, and I do care. Even when I am on a deadline, I never forget that people come first. They are the reason I am telling a story in the first place.

Present the Full Story

We, the media, are all supposed to be striving for objectivity, but I don't believe that is attainable. Journalists are just human beings shaped by their experiences, like anyone else. We make judgments simply in the selection of stories we cover in a day. For example, why does the media make a big deal out of some murders and not others? I don't think that in most cases people in the newsroom are purposefully trying to exclude or offend anyone in news coverage. I have found that people feel excluded from news coverage when we as journalists don't address that we are biased, often unconsciously biased, toward certain people, or neighborhoods, or issues.

For example, in New Orleans, shootings are very common, and typically they take place in the same neighborhoods, which tend to be lower-income areas with a majority of black residents (of course, race and poverty are tied to crime for many reasons). So when we are in the newsroom and a shooting occurs, location is usually the first piece of information we use to figure out how big of a story the shooting is. Is it in a neighborhood where we have already covered several other shootings this week? Is it another case where police have no suspect or motive? On the other hand, maybe we get word of a shooting in an area where shootings don't typically happen. Simply because the location is out of the ordinary, that shooting becomes a bigger story that gets more attention. Viewers will often question why we, as the media, give more attention to a random shooting in a tourist area than to five shootings in a crime-ridden area. And it's a valid question.

As a journalist, it's important that I always ask myself questions. Why am I covering this story differently than I covered a similar story in another area? Sometimes it is because a manager told me too, but then it is my job to use my voice and try to correct any bias that I see happening. For me, being balanced and giving viewers a complete story is not about pretending that I am not human and don't have biases. To truly be balanced, I have to recognize my biases and then realize that viewers may have the same bias. In fact, I use any bias I have to enhance my stories.

One time I did a story on a program that helps ex-offenders find jobs once they get out of prison. The program was doing some very important work, but I kept thinking that a lot of people are not going to care if a former prisoner could find a job. In fact, they may feel they don't deserve any help because they broke the law. So I made sure to ask the woman who ran the program why a person who has no connection to prisoners should care about this program, and she had a great answer. She explained that these ex-offenders were reentering society whether we liked it or not, so it is in everyone's best interest that they find jobs and get on a track to being a productive citizen. I think that a lot of people would have blown that story off because it was about former prisoners, but by anticipating that some people would be biased, I believe that I was able to show people why they should care about the story despite any judgments they had.

I always keep viewers in mind when I am putting a story together. I do feel that I owe it to viewers to provide them with a balanced story, and for me it means addressing the biases that I anticipate the public has and my own.

Make More Mistakes

I have said all along that mistakes are inevitable, and I have made some at every stage of the game. One time, when I was doing live shots for the morning show, I covered a story of a man who had drowned in Lake Pontchartrain. Two relatives showed up as crews continued to search for the body. The older gentleman told me I would have to speak to the child he was with, who was ten or eleven, because the man could not speak English. I had encountered this situation before with Spanish-speaking families. I asked the young boy why he was here and what happened. He explained that his relative (I think his cousin) was swimming when he went under the water. I asked him what his cousin was like, trying to get some basic information. He started to cry, but I asked if he wanted to keep talking. He said yes, and I asked how he felt. He broke down and the interview ended. Well, when we aired the interview, I was bashed for being so heartless and insensitive to shove the mic in this crying boy's face. The comments hurt because that was the furthest thing from the truth. I wanted to tell people that I stopped after he was visibly upset and that he told me he wanted to speak on behalf of his family. But I understood that from the outside, I looked as if I was taking advantage of this child for sound bites. I had been doing the story all morning without sound bites.

I learned that even if a child says he wants to speak in such a tragic situation, I should know better. Budding journalists will experience a lot of hard learning moments in this business, because what we do is public and we are often dealing with people in very tense situations. I was very upset about this mistake, but I had to push past it and commit to doing better next time.

13

Get a Life!

You can't have everything you want, but you can have the things that really matter to you.

Marissa Mayer

Because of the insane schedules in the newsroom, many people think we don't have lives outside of work. I certainly live a full life with my family and friends and do things that I enjoy. Most of my coworkers have families of their own and manage to get it all done. A lot of young people worry about work-life balance. They want to make sure their entire lives aren't focused on work. Even in a field as demanding as this one, it's possible to have a full life outside of the job, but I do have to be strategic to make sure that I am not consumed by my workload.

Prioritize

My social life has changed drastically since I entered the news business. Before, I was the person who could stay up all night watching TV and then sleep late into the day. Once I got into the news, I had to wake up just after one o'clock in the morning, so I couldn't stay up late on weeknights anymore. I was never the biggest fan of going out to clubs, so I never felt deprived when I started getting tired earlier and skipping out on going to bars or clubs with friends. It only took a few times for me to go with them to realize it was not worth it. While I was at work texting them about how tired I was, they were all asleep. I had to realize my circumstances were different from everyone else's. I couldn't listen to people who said that I was young and could sleep when I was dead. I like sleeping and functioning well at work. So gradually I turned down more and more invitations for nighttime events. Even on the weekends, I got used to going to bed early, so struggling to stay awake in the back of a club was not fun. On the other hand, I know many people with a newsroom schedule who carry on normal social lives, go with little to no sleep, and are happy. I certainly have gone to work with two hours of sleep after staying out late at a Mardi Gras ball or holiday party.

I don't believe that I can have it all, but as Marissa Mayer notes, I see that I can have what is most important to me. Having a fulfilling life is all about being honest with myself. I have to ignore everyone else's input about my social life and do what makes me happy—even if that is sleep. I prioritize day by day. One day, the most important thing to me might be staying up late to go a friend's party. The next day, it might be sleep, and on another, it could be staying at work late to finish a project. Taking my schedule one day at a time keeps me from getting overwhelmed.

Plan Ahead

Once I have figured out what is most important to me for the day, I figure out how to get it all done. I don't have a perfect routine down yet, but I manage to get a lot done by planning ahead. On Sunday, I look at the upcoming week and plan how my days will go. Which days will I be at work late? When can I leave on time and run errands? When do I need to take a long nap so I can stay up late?

Planning ahead helps to keep everything in balance. If I am having lunch with a friend, I try to see when I will have a quiet few days, so that I can schedule our meet-up when I don't have a pressing deadline for a story. Looking ahead is also about taking care of myself.

No amount of planning will ever lead to the perfect balance of work and life. Life happens. There are so many times that I end up dealing with something personally or professionally that throws me off balance. For instance, a relative is sick or a project comes up at work that has a quick turnaround. Suddenly, my schedule is out of whack, and I am barely sleeping, eating bad foods, and not exercising. I have learned to push through it, and then pick a day to reset. The worst thing I can do is get off track and then give up because I have messed up. The key to not becoming consumed by my crazy schedule is bouncing back after a few hard days or weeks. I have to do that to keep myself healthy.

Vacation

Tons of people claim they have too much work to do to take all of their vacation, but I am not one of those people. It's important to get away from the newsroom and live my life. If I plan ahead, there is no reason I can't take all of my vacation and get my work done. Anchors do not get overtime pay. Instead, we get "comp" (or compensatory) days for working extra hours. I make sure that I take those mental breaks, even if I do end up doing some work or checking emails while I am off. The newsroom places restrictions on vacations: no February, May, or November vacations because of sweeps rating periods. And in New Orleans, we have to worry about events such as hurricane season throwing off our plans. We have to keep all of that in mind when we plan off days for the year.

I find that often when people tell me they can't take vacation, it is not the station denying their request for off time. The issue is that they feel guilty about not doing work, even though the vacation is available for them to use. Taking time off allows me to refresh myself and come back a more productive worker. Plus, if I died tomorrow, the station would figure out a way to move forward without me. Trust me, they can survive without any employee for a few days.

Say No

The key to achieving work-life balance for me was getting used to saying no. I could not believe the number of opportunities that started coming my way simply because I was on TV. There were suddenly countless requests for emceeing events, being a celebrity judge, speaking at graduations, etc. Newsroom staffs don't have anyone to handle these requests for us, so I was spending a considerable amount of time just trying to keep track of all the phone calls and emails.

On-air talent are not paid by the station for events we attend. The majority of it is volunteer work. When I first got on TV, I tried to say yes to every request that anyone made. I was so grateful to be in my position that I wanted to give back in any way I could. It wasn't long before I was working seven days a week many weeks. I would emcee an event for hours on a Friday night, and then I would be a celebrity judge for a contest the next day.

The reporter job didn't come with a guidebook on juggling these other parts of my life. It took me nearly two years in the business to learn to say no and not feel guilty about it. Again, a fulfilling life is about prioritizing. Now, I simply decide which events are important to me and volunteer for only those.

Friends

Friends are a big part of life, and they can play a huge role in how we spend our time. I tend to make friends easily, and I've always had a lot of people whom I considered close friends. In my senior year of high school, there was a group of about seven girls whom I considered all best friends. By the end of senior year, I went to prom with only two of them by my side. Several of us were not talking to each other anymore. It all started from something so petty that to this day, I still don't know why we fell out. That experience was a rude awakening that the friends I held so close to my heart and shared so much of my life with could turn on me in a split second.

Still, I went off to college at NYU and became really close to my two roommates, who had also gone to Dominican. We were in New York without family, so they really felt like my sisters. By sophomore year, one of the girls was distancing herself and things got weird among us all. This pattern—of losing people who I imagined would be in my life forever—continued even as I entered the workforce.

I am an all-or-nothing person, so once someone shows me that they can't be trusted or that they are not hanging out with me for genuine reasons, I cut them from my life pretty abruptly. I had let go of so many friends that I started to wonder if I was the problem. In my twenties, I began to realize that part of my mistake was being too trusting. It would be great if we lived in a world where everyone is honest and only befriends others without motives. But that is just not the world we live in. There are a lot of people who were my friend because it was convenient or beneficial to them. I hadn't realized how cold and selfish people could be. I was very naïve, but by my early twenties, I began being more careful about the people I got close to.

It's important that I am careful about who I spend my time with. I like to surround myself with people who want something for themselves. Having friends who were busy pursing their dreams definitely helped me stay focused, but I also don't drop my friends if they go through a rough patch. Sometimes, it's my turn to be the inspiration. We encourage each other through the struggles, celebrate our victories, and push each other to challenge ourselves. Passion and enthusiasm are contagious. I like to be around people who inspire me through the excitement they have for their own lives. People come and go in life, and sometimes losing someone will hurt. Learning to let people go without holding grudges has helped me build the life and social circle I want. I can see now that certain people were removed from my life for a reason.

Dating

The untraditional work schedule of the newsroom can definitely impact a journalist's dating life. When most normal people would go out to dinner, I was going to bed. Dating is certainly doable. I found someone who understood and could deal with my schedule, and my job wasn't an issue at all.

When I was trying to break into the business, I wasn't worried about a relationship. I was worried only about myself. I knew that I did not want to be in a serious relationship until I landed my first reporting job. I never dated a lot anyway. But as much as I have thought about my career and professional life, I have always envisioned my future with a family of my own.

I was not the girl who was into going out on dates for a free meal. I have a lot to do to get to where I want to be. If I was not interested in someone, even one date seemed like a waste of time. I had a million more productive things I could be doing.

Once I got on TV, I did worry that someone would want to date me just because I was in the spotlight, and I met a few who did. I had to learn to really listen when people speak and trust my gut. I was also thinking that no one would tolerate my daytime naps or schedule that called for being asleep by eight o'clock at night. What if I met someone and had to relocate (which can happen in this business)? Dating was hard enough, but dating as someone in the news business adds its own unique complexities.

I met my boyfriend while I was out reporting, just a few months before I would be promoted to anchor. All of the doubts I had about making a relationship work went away because we wanted it to work. I could not be luckier. He is one of the most caring and supportive people I know—and not just to me but to everyone in his life. What really works for me is having someone who is ambitious and has his own goals and plans. Like careers, relationships are all about how much work we are willing to put in. I am dedicated to working on my personal growth, and I think the key to our relationship is being committed to working on ourselves separately and then on our relationship together. I know we are taught to find someone who completes us, but I think you should complete yourself and work on a relationship with another complete person.

14

Forget the Joneses

*Too many people spend money they haven't earned to buy
things they don't want to impress people they don't like.*
Will Rogers

Even after landing my third job in TV, I was struggling financially. One of the hardest parts of being on TV was dealing with everyone thinking I had money when I didn't. My mom and I had a good laugh when I took her to a speaking engagement with me and she overheard some young men talking about how I was a millionaire. Yes, I was on TV, but I was making an average salary. I still lived at home with my parents. I still drove my Corolla with no hubcaps. I had saved for the car while working at the event-planning company. I still had close to $60,000 in student loan debt. The great thing is that I was so used to being in a different financial situation from the people around me that I didn't cave into the pressure to keep up the image people had of me. People kept asking me when I was going to buy a new car or move away from home. None of them bothered to ask how much debt or savings I had. I realized that people who supposedly cared about me would pressure me right off a cliff.

Looking at My Reality

I was where I wanted to be and working at the number one station in our market, but I had to look at my reality. I was in a lot of debt, and even though I was in a good place professionally, I wasn't making much money at all as a traffic reporter. I started paying way more than the minimum on one of my loans, and figured if I stayed at home with my parents and kept my expenses low, I would eventually make a crack in the debt. I wanted a new car and a cute little apartment, and to be on my own, but I had to accept I just wasn't there yet, despite my position.

Getting out of debt was a challenge. I had a constant sense of restraint that felt suffocating at times. I had survived without hardly any disposable income for most of my life. I realized that making more money didn't mean that I had to spend more money. I kept living just as I did when I worked at the retail store in college, and I sent most of my paychecks to the loan companies. Of course, there were times I wasn't perfect—I spent too much money on shopping or eating out—but for the most part, I stayed focused on the bigger picture. I wanted to build my future on a solid financial foundation and not always live paycheck to paycheck.

Only I knew my real situation. No one in my immediate family owned property or anything of value. There was no emergency savings. No one in my family could buy me a car, help me pay bills, or give me a down payment on my house. And that's fine. People come from all kinds of financial backgrounds. My parents gave me the foundation so that I could do it myself. I was surprised by the number of people who would ask when I was moving out of my parents home or suggest that I buy a car. I would then find out that someone bought them a car or had a mortgage down payment waiting for them when they reached a certain point in life. I hope to do the same thing for my future children, but that's not my current life.

I am so glad I didn't fall into the trap of trying to match my lifestyle and job title. My lifestyle matches what's in my wallet. Being on TV didn't come with an automatic switch that provided a quick fix to my financial issues. I had to be honest with myself about where I was and not get swallowed up by the bright lights and encouragement to buy more clothes and a new car to match the shiny image that came with being in the limelight. It doesn't matter what anyone else is doing. I make sure my spending is in line with my goals and future vision.

Salary

Most people want a lot of money and nice things. A high-paying job is great, but I also believe we are all put on this earth with a purpose. And to fulfill that purpose, I think we have to do what we are meant to do. We are all unique and have our own set of skills and talents for a reason. They are intended to be used for a greater good. Still, it was hard for me to focus on a quest for meaning and purpose, because I didn't come from much. I wanted to follow my passions and find my purpose, but I also wanted and needed to make money. It didn't take me long to realize that I would be miserable if I chose a profession or college major solely for money. And a poor miserable person and a rich miserable person are both miserable.

The key to this challenge is finding balance. For instance, in my dream world, I would have left college and wrote a novel. There was only one problem. That plan didn't involve a steady paycheck. So I stuck with the writing idea and went in a direction that did provide steady pay.

For someone who wants to be a singer, has a lot of talent, but needs to start making money right out of college, they could major in music business. With that degree, the person opens the door to other options besides performing every night to pay their bills—which can be wonderful, but my musician friends say it's also quite unreliable.

My mom taught me so much, and among those lessons was learning to listen to myself. There is a reason I feel compelled to write. There's a reason someone else feels compelled to sing or study medicine, and I believe we should follow those natural urges. I did follow my urge to write, just not in the sense I had envisioned. The world praises certain careers and professions—such as doctors and lawyers—because they are known to come with a great paycheck. But trust me, there are lots of people who listened to everyone except themselves, went to medical school or law school to chase a paycheck, and aren't making money. Someone out there is doing a terrible job as a lawyer, but maybe they would have been better off on a career path that traditionally doesn't make a lot of money. I find that when I am passionate about something, I am willing to put in the hard work to figure out how it can make money.

Salary is important, though. I wanted to get out of debt and make money as soon as possible. Being an English major and going into news wasn't exactly the most profitable plan, but I knew that I would work hard until I was making what I wanted. I never hesitated about going into the field because of money, even though I was broke.

Many people get their foot in the door in the news industry making just eight dollars an hour as a desk assistant. I started at ten dollars an hour as an associate producer. I interned for college credit, which meant I didn't get any money. Thankfully, most internships are paid now, but I do know of some companies where students still get college credit instead of wages. The low or no wages favors the privileged. I did not even have a car when I first started working at WWL. My mom dropped me off and picked me up, and then I walked across the street to my second job. It was only because of that second job in event planning that I was able to buy a car.

But I found myself working beside people making the same amount who had cars and apartments or houses, and I was living at home buried in debt. I knew that I couldn't get distracted trying to keep up with people around me.

Many of them had more support from their parents. I was doing a lot on my own, so I was really building from the ground up. Still, the numbers didn't discourage me from entering the business. I let them motivate me to keep moving up. I didn't sit around waiting for a promotion. I took the initiative to talk to my boss about my future.

No matter what industry you work in or how much money you make, you will have to carve out your own path financially to reach your goals. Don't buy a car just because everyone else buys a car. I have learned that a lot of the people buying the stuff I want can't afford it either. When I do get caught up and buy clothing or some unnecessary material item, even if I am happy about it in the moment, in the long run I usually regret deviating from my plan. I figured out early in my professional life that I needed to make a good salary to reach my financial goals, but I also needed to be constantly conscious of how I spent my money to make sure that I was using that hard-earned money to gain financial stability.

15
Hosting My Own Show

The most courageous act is still to think for yourself.
Aloud.

Coco Chanel

Establishing a Brand

I had been reporting for just over a year when opportunity knocked once again. One of our early morning show anchors had a baby and, not long after, decided to leave the show. Not long before she left, the station had created a show for her called *The 504*. I was promoted to anchor and, since the former anchor had her own show, that fell under my responsibility too. I barely had experience on TV, so taking on the roles of morning anchor and show host all at once was a lot. But I was too focused on getting the work done to be overwhelmed. I immediately started writing ideas for the show I would host. When my news director, Bill, called me into the office to tell me the show was mine, he also told me that the only other person on my team would be one producer. Since I would have only one team member, I knew instantly that I wanted to work with Caegan Moore. She was an associate producer who actually trained me when I started at the station, and she was producing shows but was part time. She is creative and a hard worker, and I knew that she would do some fun things with the show. Bill hadn't considered her, but he told me he would try to make it work. There I was, accidentally negotiating again. And it could not have worked out better.

Humble Beginnings

The original *The 504*, with the original anchor, was nothing like what airs now. The former producer and anchor team was going for a more serious, news-like format. Sometimes they would air extended interviews with guests who had been on the morning show. The first time I had a conversation with

Bill about the show, he said he envisioned something similar to what they were already doing, a long-format show with interviews on serious topics. We were already doing four and a half hours of morning news, and I wanted to give people something different. And even though Bill had ideas about what he wanted for the show, he provided me with a rare opportunity to make it my own. There was no other person on air at the station who had the power to just do whatever they wanted with their air time. I didn't even have that power as a new morning show anchor, even though that was the more high-profile position because the morning show has a lot more viewers.

I knew that the creative freedom the station was giving me was powerful. I put a lot of thought into what I wanted to put on TV. When we first started taping shows, I was really focused on communities that were being neglected, so we did segments featuring missing person cases, positive untold stories in our area, and topics such as local HIV rates. We followed that vision for nearly an entire year, but I was not happy with the work we were doing. It just felt too much like what was already happening on other news shows in the market. And our strategy of randomly choosing a different topic to focus on each night made the show feel unnatural and oftentimes very forced. For instance, we would want to talk about a big conversation happening around the nation, but we couldn't because we had boxed ourselves in by deciding that our theme for the night was, for example, suicide. The other problem with choosing a random topic to focus on for the night was finding guests to cover the topic. It was often difficult to find experts on the issues I wanted to discuss.

Time for Change

Quite honestly, for those first two years, I was not happy with the show at all. I thought it was flat-out boring, and I did not have the resources or team to make the show exactly as I wanted to. Eventually, I got fed up doing a show that I was not proud of. Caegan and I were working so hard. People were saying we were doing a good job, but some were merely impressed that we managed to get the show on air five nights a week. I had higher expectations for us than just being on air. I needed to be satisfied with the content we were producing each night. We started brainstorming ways to make the show easier to book and more interesting. Every Thursday night, we aired an episode that we were calling "Hot Talk" back then. It has now developed into our "Hot Mess" night, where we discuss the craziest stories we find in a week. From the beginning, we brought on two local radio hosts, Stevie G and TPot, and a third wild-card guest to weigh in on trending topics. On those nights, the show felt fresh, young, and entertaining. I cannot thank Stevie G and TPot enough for their dedication to the show. They really add a fun spark, and I wanted that fun vibe to be our defining feature.

Since Thursday nights already captured the vibe I wanted for the show, I was trying to think of practical ways to replicate that vibe other nights of the week. It took lots of trial and error. But the beauty of having so much creative license was that there was no manager breathing down our backs or critiquing how the shows went. We had a rare opportunity to learn on TV, with nothing to lose. The show has grown tremendously from those days of doing random segments or serious interviews. As far as the stories we cover now, we learned to have a more narrow focus so that viewers know what to expect each night.

My vision was to have a show where people come to be entertained, and now we have that. We cover entertainment and lifestyle news, with a focus on trending topics. The show has a panel of guests every night except for Friday, when we highlight local musicians. After I was clear about the content of the show, my new vision needed a new look to go with it.

Ask and You Shall Receive

The content wasn't the only issue I had with *The 504*. When I first started the show, *The 504*'s set was the same as the news set. So practically anywhere I sat, the WWL letters were plastered somewhere near me. Our show, however, was on an entirely different channel, WUPL. To make things even more confusing, people knew me as an anchor on WWL. Our guests and viewers were constantly confused when it came time to find the show on TV because different cable service providers aired the station on different channels. The news set didn't feel like the right atmosphere for the more lighthearted, entertaining vibe I was going for anyway. I really wanted us to have our own set, so I kept mentioning it to Tod Smith, the station's general manager. He has always been supportive of my team and appreciates that we are trying to build something from the ground up.

I had Caegan reach out to West Elm, a national furniture company that she had booked for some segments on the show in the past, and ask if they would sponsor our set. It was that simple. They would provide the furniture for the set and accessorize it. And to be clear, there was no budget for this or anything for *The 504* for that matter. They were giving us the entire set for free. All we had to do was tell people where we got all of our cute furniture.

That win set an entire revamp of the show into motion. I shutdown production for most of the summer, and we aired reruns. I wanted everything to have a new, cohesive identity, including the theme music, logo, and set. We spent months going through logo versions. My boyfriend suggested we make the logo look like tiles on some New Orleans' streets that spell out the street name. It was the perfect fit. We spent a lot of time going over furniture options and even debated shades of aqua for the walls. In the end, it was worth it. The show finally felt as if it had its own identity.

My Workload

Having my own show is amazing, but the part that people don't get to see is that off air, it requires a ton of work to get done. On the morning show, we have an executive producer and five or more producers, who work behind the scenes. They figure out what the segments will be, book them, and print out information to give us anchors to prepare for the interview. On the morning show, I pitch ideas and give input, but the foundation of the show is laid out by a team of producers. *The 504* was an entirely different story. Caegan and I were a two-person team, carrying the workload of about five people.

I was anchoring the morning show and then switching gears to get ready to tape *The 504*. The show airs weeknights at nine, but it is actually taped around ten in the morning, right after the morning show. Not only was I hosting, but I was running *The 504*'s social media accounts, coming up with segment ideas, writing the entire show, helping book guests, and constantly creating ideas for content. Caegan was doing most of the booking for the show, coordinating with guests (which could mean managing a dozen emails to get everything set up for their appearance on the show), editing all of the video and sound that went into the show, and trying to find interesting guests and topics to fill fifteen to twenty segments a week.

For the other news shows, the producers don't do the editing, the hosts don't do the majority of the writing, and there are social media managers who do nothing but post on social media. No one was making me do all of this work. I could be a diva and just show up for the show without helping, but the only person I would be hurting is myself. After the first few episodes, I started writing the scripts because Caegan was swamped. It turned out I loved writing the show, because, then, everything I say is in my voice. On the morning show, someone is writing everything for me unless I specifically go into the computer and change a script. I just feel more connected to stories and deliver them better when I have written them. And if the show was bad, no one was going to call the producer to complain. All of the criticism falls on me. I refer to myself as the host and executive producer of *The 504* because at the end of the day, I am not just the host. I oversee everything that happens on the show, mainly to protect my brand. *The 504* is my show in the sense that I am the only face associated with it, and I want it to reflect me.

I don't get overtime when I stay late to develop segments, help my producer book guests, or write the show. I do these things because I really believe in the work we are doing. I am proud of what we are building, and it takes a lot of focus to work hard on something that is still new. It is very rewarding, and I love watching my ideas unfold into segments on television. "Working for free" didn't end with my first job, and I don't think it will until I make it to the ultimate vision of what I want for myself in life. I will always have to work more than is required—and, oftentimes, more than anyone notices—to keep moving forward.

The revamp really made me feel more optimistic about the show, but even with a clearer vision and unique logo, Caegan and I were frustrated, exhausted, and still finding it impossible to execute our perfect vision many days, because we literally didn't have enough hours in a day. I called another meeting with Tod and Bill. I said that I appreciated all they had done so far to support my efforts to improve the show, but I still needed more help. They said they would work on it. Bill eventually took a new route professionally, which took him away from the station. We got a new news director, Keith Esparros. Even though he was new, I had the same old agenda when it came to improving *The 504*.

After three years of doing the show, my managers finally gave me permission to hire a production assistant. We wasted no time finding the third member of our team, who would edit the show. Josh Detiege brought a fresh eye to our work, and he is a great photographer. Now, I always have someone on hand to take amazing pictures and shoot stories with. It didn't take long for the station to hire Josh as a full-time photographer. His addition to the team has allowed us to take our game to the next level. I am extremely grateful for a hardworking team. I may be the face of the show, but it is impossible to do a show alone. Even with Josh on the team, we are still limited in how much we can get done.

My day starts at two thirty, to wake up and anchor the morning show at four thirty. By the time we finish taping *The 504*, it's eleven or eleven thirty in the morning, and I still need to write scripts for the next day's show. That way, when I go home, the team can format the show for TV, create any graphics we need, and edit video. So if I want to go out and shoot a story, I would be starting after noon, already eight hours after I get to work. I don't mind

Hosting The 504. (Photo by Josh Detiege)

Hosting The 504. (Photo by Josh Detiege)

The 504 *team: production assistant Josh Detiege (center) and producer Caegan Moore (right).* (Photograph by author)

working overtime for a special project or story, but it's just not realistic or healthy to regularly stay behind and shoot more stories, even though I love doing stories outside of the station. We do take breaks from taping some days, and I try to use those days to shoot pieces outside of the station.

Social media takes up an insane amount of my day as well. People assume that someone handles my social media accounts, but it's just me. I spend hours a day posting on social media, creating posts, and editing pictures for my personal accounts and for the show's accounts. The social media work for *The 504* could be a job all by itself. Thankfully, Josh helps with that, so I have a little bit of relief.

Even though we have grown tremendously, we are not done. We are always trying something new in an effort to be more entertaining, engaging, and in touch with our viewers. And apparently, it's working. In 2016, *The 504* took home the Press Club of New Orleans's award for best talk show.

Using My Voice

It was not a smooth transition from reporting to anchoring and hosting. I moved up in the ranks so fast that I had to learn as I went along. I was just getting into the swing of hosting *The 504*. During this time, I interviewed a local professor on the minimum wage debate. I had researched the issue, but the conversation went in a direction I had not expected. He started spewing all kinds of racist comments, and when he said, "Historically, black people have low production rates," I was so shocked that I did not even know how to respond. I sat there quietly and thanked him when the interview was over. But I was extremely disappointed in my performance. I was caught off guard. I should have challenged him about the source of his information. A viewer sent me an email the next day saying he was disappointed with the interview and felt that I could have done a better job challenging the nonsense. I could only agree and told him to keep watching because I would do better next time.

The best part about having my own show is developing ideas and watching them come to life. I have had to accept that sometimes the ideas work and sometimes they don't. I get a lot of great feedback from people who are happy the show spotlights so many positive locals doing cool things. I also have to be thick-skinned and know that everyone won't agree with what I choose to talk about or how. Since the show is entertainment based, I often take a biased stance, putting my opinions out there on trending topics. I have to be strong, knowing my guests and viewers won't always agree with me. The goal of my show is not to have everyone agree. It is to spark conversations. When

My dad appeared on The 504 *for a Father's Day cooking segment.* (Photograph by author)

it's time to decide what to cover, I always explore both sides of the story and think about the conversations that could follow.

Overall, there have been way more good times than bad. I have interviewed big celebrities like Hulk Hogan; the hosts of the daytime talk show *The Real*, including two of my favorites, Tamera Mowry and Adrienne Bailon; actor Morris Chestnut; actress Regina Hall; and the list goes on. One of the highlights has been having my dad on for Father's Day episodes. My dad and I are a lot alike. He loves to entertain and have a good time. The first time he came on the show, he did a cooking segment. My dad is an amazing cook, always whipping up some new dish for me to try. The next year, he showed up dirty shirt and all (that's my dad), and we had a blast talking about some current events going on.

For Aspiring Entertainment Journalists

When people ask me what my dream job is, I always say to host a talk show. And usually they reply, "You already have a show." I do and I am extremely grateful for it. But as I pointed out in the beginning of the book, there are cooks at McDonald's and then there are chefs at five-star restaurants. Yes, they can both say they are cooks, but there's a huge difference. So, yes, I have my own show, but this is not a national show. It can only be seen in New

Orleans, and it is on a channel that is still developing a brand, as opposed to a major network that people are familiar with and are already eager to watch.

I meet many aspiring journalists who tell me they want a show like *The 504*. There is nothing wrong with that, but I am honest with them about how getting this show was happenstance, and that my paycheck comes from being a WWL anchor. I tell these aspiring entertainment reporters to go to L.A. and put themselves in a space where there are tons of great entertainment jobs. Don't go work at a news station expecting to be an entertainment reporter. It's just not a thing in most local newsrooms. *The 504* would not even be an entertainment show if my managers had not given me free creative license to do whatever I wanted with it.

More Opportunities, More Caution

New Orleans bounce artist Big Freedia was one of my dream guests. Freedia was gaining national attention for her music when I first reached out. Surprisingly, Freedia came on the show. I loved her even more in person. Freedia became a huge supporter and came on several times as the years passed. In our third year, she was filming her reality show on FUSE and asked to tape for her show while we did an episode of *The 504*.

The team was so excited. We couldn't wait to be on national TV. We created some fun game segments and cooking segments. We wanted the show to be special, since it would be seen nationally. The day before Big Freedia was set to come on the show, WWL's investigative team broke the news that Freedia was facing a federal indictment for unlawful use of the Housing Choice Voucher Program Section 8. Management had some concerns about us going forward with the fun show. We decided that we would still do the show, but I would address the indictment before we moved on to the rest of the fun episode that we had been planning.

I am not a reporter who loves to ambush or shock interviewees. I always warn them if I am going to ask them something controversial. So I pulled Freedia aside and explained that I had to ask about the indictment. Freedia told me that she didn't want to talk about it. I am a journalist first, so I could not sit there and act as if I didn't know that she was yesterday's biggest headline. I explained to Freedia that I promised my managers that I would at least ask her to address the indictment. I told Freedia that she could answer however she chose and then we would move on. She said ok.

The episode on Big Freedia's show aired months later, and before I even saw it, I was getting messages on social media about how I had betrayed

Interviewing bounce artist Big Freedia. (Photograph by author)

Freedia and asked her a question that she told me not to. I was shocked, but I instantly understood. The show had been edited to look as if I had surprised Freedia with the question about the indictment. They never aired the conversation we had where I told Freedia exactly what I was going to do. I was disappointed in myself for being involved with reality TV. It's all about drama, but I never imagined that something so small could have been twisted. I have no hard feelings against Freedia. That's how reality TV works. I have interviewed her since, and we've laughed about the crazy people who attacked me on social media after watching the interview. The situation did teach me that I was going to have to be more careful about the opportunities I accepted as I moved forward and more opportunities came my way.

16
At the Anchor Desk

An educated man should know everything about something and something about everything.

C. V. Wedgwood

I wanted to be an anchor by the time I turned thirty years old, but as I am writing this book, I still have a few years to go before I hit the big 3-0. To practice anchoring, Bill let me fill in during the four thirty half hour of the morning show when one of the anchors was off, and then I would start doing traffic reports at five in the morning. When I was told that I would be promoted to anchor full time, it was pretty surreal, but the other anchors at the station supported me. They were all pretty legendary in New Orleans, so their approval meant a lot.

Impostor Syndrome

I was extremely excited to take the position, but I was also overwhelmed. I had been on TV for about two years when I was promoted to anchor. Most of the people who work at WWL have decades of experience in the news business, and I was promoted over some of those people. There was a voice inside me saying, "You're amazing. You've been working hard. You have a special gift and God put a news director in your life who recognized that gift. You were given this amazing opportunity, and you will not take it for granted." I never said it out loud, but there was also a small part of me that felt as if I was just lucky and wasn't really supposed to be in that position.

I am fascinated when I learned about other people's professional journeys. Now, I know it is not uncommon, especially for women, to experience impostor syndrome, a fear that you aren't really supposed to be where you are and that people will find out you are a fraud. I thought, "One day, they are going to realize that I am not as talented or capable as the people I co-anchor with, and then I will have to find another job." It took a long time for this feeling to go away. The more I was challenged and did well, the more I realized that I was actually really good at what I was doing and that I was not there because of luck.

Anchoring versus Reporting

Sounding Natural

Anchoring presents different challenges from reporting. In a typical newscast, everything is written for us by a producer, so we just have to deliver the information, which sounds simple. Technically, we are just reading, but that would be like saying a photographer "just" takes pictures, when we know an experienced photographer has techniques that can make a picture look more amazing than if the average person took the picture. In the same way, there is more to anchoring than just reading. We have to sound comfortable with the material, connect with it, and be in control of it.

Being comfortable means reading the scripts before we go on air. Someone else wrote it, so we have to make sure it flows and sounds like something we would actually say. It is easier to sound natural when we report on a story because we gathered the information and wrote the story. When we anchor, we read dozens of stories in a day, and we do not have time to do extensive research or gather information firsthand. We also want to connect with these stories and not just read them like a random set of facts on a page. We ask ourselves "Who would care about this story?" "What's the right tone?" "Do the words match the tone?" For instance, imagine if an anchor wrote, "Sad news—water bills are increasing." It's not wrong, but it's also not appropriate for the situation. We have to take the time to tweak the scripts that are written for us so that we can deliver them in a compelling way. If I don't understand something in a script, I ask the producer questions or look up the story for clarity.

Another big struggle for me has been pronunciations. There were so many common place names, personal names, and words—especially in international stories—that I just did not know how to say. Imagine being on TV making up words! Thankfully, my much more experienced coworkers never got tired of me yelling across the studio to ask them how to say a word. For the first two years, I kept a pronunciation list in my phone, and every time I had to ask one of my co-anchors to tell me how a word was pronounced, I put it on the list.

Accountability

As an anchor, I am held accountable by viewers for factors that are out of my control. My producer may make a mistake, but if I read it, I am blamed for the mistake. I have to be familiar with the news so that I can read scripts and fix incorrect or misleading text. Being an anchor also makes me an authority. If I misspeak, I address it. If I feel that a story should or shouldn't be in a newscast, I say so, because I am the one who will have to defend anything that happens on the air.

There was a time when our producers would write stories about fast food all the time. McDonald's got a new burger, Burger King has all-day breakfast—blah, blah, blah. It was as if our news show had turned into a fast-food commercial. I am not a fan of fast food. First, it's not fast. Second, it's barely food. I didn't like reading the stories and didn't think it had much value to our viewers. I spoke to my executive producer, and she agreed that those stories didn't belong in our show.

I also have to make sure that I support everything that comes out of my mouth. In one instance, a producer kept referring to the Affordable Care Act as "Obamacare." Obamacare is a nickname for the act, and sometimes, it was used in a demeaning matter. It is more appropriate for journalists to use the proper name for the legislation. In another case, in which we covered U.S. riots over the shooting death of another unarmed black men, one of our producers wrote about a "violent night" of protests. I had been following the story, and I hadn't seen any reason to classify the riots as violent. I asked her what she was referring to, and she couldn't justify her use of the word. I took it out of the script and told her not to write it in there for me to read anymore. During times like those, I think back to being called a refugee by news anchors during Katrina. Someone incorrectly labeled us, and then everyone just followed along. I try to challenge the norm and make sure that I am not using a term just because other news outlets are using it. I ask instead, "Is it accurate?" "Is it insensitive for no reason?"

Knowing a Little Bit about Everything

When I was reporting, I was able to focus on just one story at a time. When I started anchoring, I had to know a little bit about everything going on that day. The most difficult thing about being an anchor is ad-libbing. On a typical day, the show is scripted for us, and we do make tweaks. However, if there is breaking news or special live coverage of an event, sometimes there are no scripts, and we are on live TV filling hours of airtime. That's why it is so important to keep up with the news.

The first time I was faced with this situation, I was on air without any of my co-anchors when President Obama was speaking at Nelson Mandela's funeral. The producer told me that they were not sure exactly when the president would speak. We would air President Obama's speech live when he appeared at the podium, and I would ad-lib until he spoke, which could be in five seconds or five minutes. Luckily, it was about thirty seconds, but I had taken the time to make some notes about the funeral and Mandela's life. I was intimidated when I first started. I was quietly panicking about how long we would be on air, and the producer was constantly giving me directions in my ear about what to do next. It was stressful, but research and preparation got me through.

Working as a Team

And speaking of getting through, I cannot emphasize enough how important it was to have a team that supported me. I had dreamed of working at WDSU after I interned there, and I was disappointed when they didn't hire me. It wasn't until I saw how things played out at WWL that I knew I had landed in the right place. WWL proved to be the best learning environment for me, because the anchor team was made up of veterans who already were local superstars. They didn't have to compete with anyone. Mike started at the station the same year I was born, and Sally-Ann Roberts and Eric Paulsen have been there for more than forty years.

The huge gap in our years of experience was very intimidating. They were all absolute pros. I know that I would not have been as successful in my position without them. Yes, they were helping me pronounce words, but their support went beyond that.

Mike Hoss is no longer my co-anchor. He surprised us all and left the station after the end of my three-year contract. We anchored together from four thirty to six in the morning, before Sally and Eric are on air. He helped me get the co-anchor position by critiquing my work and encouraging me along the way. He taught me so much about the business and handling myself on TV that I still have him listed as professor in my phone. He's ready for anything. He always did more research than needed, and he always had a plan. That man had a second job teaching me some of the basics of life on that desk during commercial breaks, and the best part of our relationship is

Anchoring the news. (Photograph by author)

My first morning show anchor team: Mike Hoss (top left), Eric Paulsen (top right), and Sally-Ann Roberts (right). (Photograph by author)

Election coverage with my former co-anchor, Mike Hoss. (Photograph by author)

Anchoring with Eric Paulsen and Sally-Ann Roberts. (Photograph by author)

that he is open to learning too. He quickly became the star of my social media videos. I am proud to say I made him go viral more than once. People just couldn't get enough of him dancing. We brought in millions of views online and even landed on the popular entertainment website World Star Hip Hop because of his dancing. Mike is a friend for life, and I am forever grateful for his guidance on the anchor desk.

Eric Paulsen and I have become known for fighting with each other on TV. People often stop me in the street to say that they love how I keep Eric in his place. When I began tuning into the news in college, every morning, I would watch him anchoring with Sally before I went to school. In real life, we get along like brother and sister. He says he only teases people he likes, so I guess I should take it as a compliment that we fight constantly. Eric gives me a lot of great life advice off camera. One day, I was anchoring, and I was wearing a surgical boot on my foot because of a minor foot procedure. I was very upset because I had asked the directors not to show me on camera with the boot, and they did it anyway. The directors were making a big deal about having to work around me, when I was the one who'd had surgery. Eric pulled me aside to calm me down and gave me advice for handling such a situation in the future.

I have a wonderful financial adviser, but I call Eric my financial adviser too. He is very open to talking about money, and I soak up a lot of financial knowledge from talking with him. And I will never forget that he encouraged me to just be myself when I first went on air. He is a great example of knowing your worth and demanding respect. I am happy to call him a friend too.

And then there is Sally. Sally is just as viewers see her on TV: motivational and uplifting. She is the ultimate encourager. She encouraged me to write this book. I told her that one day I dreamed of writing a book, and she insisted that I start now. She told me to start by writing one page a day, and even though I wasn't convinced that it would go anywhere, I did it. She took me out to lunch for a long talk before I started anchoring on the morning show and continues to be someone I can go to for advice or just to talk. Sally will tell me if she feels as if I should be doing something else to further my career. She is extremely well respected at the station, and she was a big supporter of me getting my own show.

I can only imagine what it would have been like to come into the business with people who were not as supportive—or, even worse, who wanted to sabotage me. I know that I was blessed to have joined a team that has been more than willing to help the next wave of journalists coming through our station. It has been amazing to share so many experiences with them on TV, but the greatest gift is being able to call them mentors and friends off air.

Morning News Is Fun

I love working in morning news, and it's the only shift I have ever worked in the newsroom. As an intern, I worked the morning shift because I could get a lot done and it worked with my school schedule. Then, when I applied for the associate producer position at WWL, it just happened to be a morning show position. I never left mornings.

Morning news is very different from evenings. The evening news anchors are in the studio for a half hour at a time together. Our anchor team is together for four and half hours every morning. That's some intense bonding time. Our early morning crew—with Laura Buchtel doing the weather, Tamica Lee doing traffic, and Mike Hoss and I co-anchoring—made work feel like a party every day. We called ourselves the AmFam (short for morning family), and we had a chemistry that people could feel through the TV screen. Whether we were fighting or laughing, everything that happened between us on TV was real. I am grateful to have been in such a fun and supportive environment when I was coming into my own as an anchor. I had a safe space to grow, and

Catching a huge fish during a fishing segment for the morning show. (Photograph by author)

people to turn to when I made mistakes or was being criticized. They have all left the station now for unrelated reasons, but we remain friends. Now, I am strong and more confident in my skills, and I know that I could anchor with anyone and be myself.

Since the morning show is so long, we also cover a lot more in a day than the evening shows do. We have serious and breaking news stories, but we also do lifestyle segments such as cooking and working out. It allows us to showcase our personalities in a way that the later newscasts just don't allow. I capitalize on the fun by making videos on my phone for social media and editing them.

News in New Orleans

News content varies by city. In New Orleans, violence is a huge problem, so we cover a lot of crime. Often, we start the newscast with back-to-back stories about shootings. Political corruption is also a major issue in New Orleans. We are also constantly talking about street repair projects to fix our pothole-ridden roads.

There's lots of bad to cover, but with all of that, we still find a million reasons to celebrate. And we often integrate those celebrations into our newscasts. For example, we do a live preview at the start of what locals call Jazz Fest (technically, the New Orleans Jazz and Heritage Festival), which brings musicians from all over the world to New Orleans for two weekends of epic outdoor concerts. We air our regular newscast on Mardi Gras day, and then at nine in the morning, when we would usually go off air, we put on costumes and report live from different parade routes around the city. During these broadcasts, I have been Superwoman; Rocky of Rocky and Bullwinkle; and my favorite, "Sheyonce," my rendition of pregnant Beyonce at the 2017 Grammys. That costume got me national attention on several websites. Our executive producer, Dominic Massa, helped me pull the idea together, along with Shel Roumillat, a supertalented costume maker who is dating one of our WWL photographers. She made a version of the intricate headpiece that Beyonce wore and took the costume to the next level.

A Day in the Life

My day begins around 2:40 a.m. Our morning show begins at four thirty, which means there's no such thing as running five minutes late for work. The show is live. We are either there, or there is no one to read the news. That's

Live Mardi Gras coverage with Mike Hoss. I was Glinda the Good Witch from the Wizard of Oz. *He wore his iconic moose costume.* (Photograph by author)

enough pressure to keep me from oversleeping. There's also no such thing as a "normal" shift in a newsroom. Even if someone is scheduled to work a regular nine-to-five shift, it is not uncommon to work overtime often.

When I was hired as an associate producer, I came in at one thirty in the morning. Many people tell me that they wouldn't be able to do that. If you would have asked me before I did it, I would have said the same thing. I loved sleeping. Like everyone else, I get up, start moving, and have my own tricks for staying awake. Most people chug coffee. I unfortunately cannot stomach the taste, but I cannot live without green tea. I always eat breakfast before we do the show, but typical breakfast foods like pancakes and oatmeal have mostly been eliminated from my diet. It's harder to wake up if I eat really late, so sometimes, I just eat dinner before the show in the morning. Even if I do eat dinner, I still wake up craving meatballs and spaghetti or red beans and rice instead of waffles, maybe because it's still dark outside. So it is not uncommon for me to eat red beans and rice at four a.m. before I go on air. By the time the show is over, I want lunch, and then I go home and eat another early dinner-like meal.

As for sleep, I don't get much. Since I started working in TV, I knew that I wasn't sleeping much, but my boyfriend bought me an activity tracker that served as a daily reminder that I was sleeping only three to five hours a night. Daily naps have become a part of my routine, as if I am back in kindergarten. I still don't make the recommended eight-hour mark, but I am trying.

This work schedule has challenged everything I ever knew to be normal. Everyone's schedules and tasks in the newsroom differ each day because we all have different responsibilities. Just because two people are on the same show or in the same position does not mean that they work the same hours or have the same responsibilities each day. My schedule differs drastically from everyone else in the newsroom because I have my own show, *The 504.* Also, there really is no such thing as a typical day because our schedules depend on the news. If there's a massive fire, instead of being behind the desk anchoring, I may be sent into the field, and my co-anchor may stay behind the desk. Or I may be working on a special shoot after the show, so I stay a few hours later in the day to get it done. But here is what my schedule looks like on most days:

My Typical Schedule

2:40 a.m. Wake up

Unfortunately, I discovered the snooze button once I got this job, but after about ten alarms, I eventually get up.

3:30 a.m. Arrive at the station

I have to proofread scripts, correct errors, and rewrite anything that isn't my style. Our producers work overnight to get the scripts written for the show. Anchors and reporters do our own hair and makeup. Somewhere in there, I take a moment to drink green tea and grab something to eat.

4:25 a.m. Head to the studio for mic check

We have to put on our mics, which can be difficult for the ladies, depending on the outfit, and our earpieces so that the producers can talk to us during the show. They tell us about any changes that might happen and give us countdowns so that we know when we are going back on air. It's normal for us to take more or less of the scheduled time discussing a story. But the show has to end at a specific time, so the producers have to make changes as we go to shorten the show or add time to it. For instance, they will say don't read story A6 about the event this weekend, to make more time in the show. Yes, sometimes people are talking to us while we are talking to viewers.

4:30 a.m. Show starts

4:30 a.m. – 6:00 a.m. Anchor with co-anchor

When I first started, Mike Hoss and I would co-anchor from four thirty to six. As I am writing this, the search is underway for my new co-anchor. All of the scripts aren't written when we come in, so that means we spend commercials breaks reading recently written scripts and editing to stay on top of things. We also look up more information on stories, in case we need to spend extra time talking about them. If Mike were on vacation, I would anchor the hour and a half by myself.

6:00 a.m. – 9:00 a.m. Our main anchors arrive

For the rest of the show, four anchors take turns reading stories, and there are weather and traffic reports. So most of the time, there are long breaks between the times I am on air. On a typical day, I use this extra time to write the scripts for my show, *The 504*. There are times when my co-anchor or I am sent to cover other stories, so we are in the field for the rest of the show. If one of the main anchors is off, I may spend the entire four and half hours on air.

9:00 a.m. – 10:00 a.m. Finish scripts for my show

I have an hour between the taping of the morning show and *The 504*. I use that time to do any last-minute tasks I need to for that day's taping of *The 504* and get any updates from my producer. I also try to finish writing the next day's scripts, so that I am done with most of my work by the time we are done taping the morning show.

10:00 a.m. – 11:30 a.m. Tape *The 504*

The show doesn't actually air until nine in the evening.

11:30 a.m. – 1:00 p.m. Work on the next episode of my show

There are so many different variables—including breaking news, last-minute changes to my show, or a colleague on vacation—that affect how long my day is, but I try to leave the newsroom by one o'clock every afternoon if nothing special is going on, for my sanity. My team for *The 504* works a normal day shift, so there are often emails to answer or issues to resolve long after my day technically ends. I also spend most nights working on new ideas for the show, so I feel as if I am constantly working or connected. Getting away from my desk at a reasonable time helps me to recharge, even though I always end up working from home later.

Beyond the Desk

Even once I leave work, there are often community obligations outside the newsroom. I see it as part of my job to be involved in the community. I make it a point to speak to schools that ask me to tell students about my job. I give graduation speeches and words of encouragement at honor ceremonies. When I first started doing this, I was nervous, because the speeches were often twenty-five to thirty minutes long, but I thought back to the Soledad speeches that I had transcribed and used them as a guide. I also have served as an emcee for many nonprofits events. I have given testimonies about my story to church groups. I've gone on the radio to promote my show. Sometimes, I've had to shoot promotion photos for the station. The point is, there is a lot going on that doesn't specifically fall in an eight-hour day.

I enjoy reporting live, but I also like staying in the studio to anchor. My schedule gives me the opportunity to do both. Sometimes, my assignments have even taken me out of town. I was sent to Houston, Texas, for storm coverage after some historic flooding hit the area in June 2015. I went with a photographer, and we helped another TEGNA-owned station, KHOU. In August 2015, the station sent me to Dallas, Texas, to interview Stephen Colbert

Riding as the grand marshal in the Krewe of Oshun with my boyfriend, 2015. (Photograph by author)

Visiting a class at Mahalia Jackson Elementary School. (Photograph by author)

ahead of his debut on *The Late Show with Stephen Colbert*. In January 2016, Screen Gems, a film production company, invited me to attend a Los Angeles press junket, an event where they bring a bunch of media representatives together to interview the stars of a film and, sometimes, the people who made the film. (I flew in, watched the movies, did the interviews the next day, and then flew home. I didn't get a chance to see anything in L.A., even though it was my first time there. I went back later to sightsee.)

Sometimes, cool non-work-related opportunities come my way because I work at WWL. One of the highlights of my life was riding as the grand marshal in a Mardi Gras parade. In February 2015, my boyfriend and I rode with the Krewe of Oshun. For those who don't know, "grand marshal" is an honorary title given by a Mardi Gras krewe (the name for the groups who organize the parades) to the person who will lead their parade. I had dreamed of riding on a float since I was a little girl, and it came true in a way that was even better than I ever planned it, because I never imagined I'd be leading the parade.

17
Being a Woman in the Industry

Women need to shift from thinking "I'm not ready to do that" to thinking "I want to do that—and I'll learn by doing it."

Sheryl Sandberg, *Lean In*

In this book, I have shared a lot of the observations that I have made through being in the workforce for several years. One of the most alarming things I have noticed is the difference in how men and women behave at work. Women tend to apologize unnecessarily, doubt themselves more, and downplay their accomplishments. The revelation was huge for me, because I realized I was doing it too.

Giving Myself Credit

My journey to the anchor desk happened so quickly that I couldn't believe how the odds kept working in my favor. When people would ask me how I did it, I would tell them I was lucky. Others were quick to tell me that I was lucky. But Kim told me that luck didn't deserve all the credit. She made me realize that someone else could have been given the same opportunities and not have worked as hard to capitalize on them. I also realized that I was downplaying the work that I did and the decisions I made that got me to where I am.

The quote "The harder I work, the luckier I get" truly reflects my life. I started to wonder if those same opportunities and jobs would have kept falling in my lap if I had not been grinding. I don't think they would have. From my experience, luck comes when I am in motion. It wasn't going to come and chase me down. I had to run to it. And the key there is running. When I am running full speed toward my goals, I do find that opportunities keep coming my way.

Stepping up Confidently

I talked to many other women, across different fields, who were attributing their wins in life to luck and were filled with self-doubt. Men at the same skill level seemed to shout their successes to the world and take the credit for every little thing that was going right in their lives. I had to get used to talking about my strengths and accomplishments. In my mind, I was ready to take on any challenge, but I never wanted to come off as cocky or over-exaggerate my abilities. So when I spoke, I focused on my doubts and shortcomings, instead of elaborating on my strengths. I wanted to be humble. I needed to trust myself enough to speak about what I was capable of doing. Otherwise, how would anyone know? I have learned it's okay to say, "Hey, I'm a really good writer" and not worry about sounding cocky. Eventually, I realized the power of taking credit for my success. It showed that I was capable of handling even bigger opportunities.

Support Other Women

I am grateful to have had relationships with wonderful women such as Soledad, Kim, and my mom, who operate like bosses. They take credit for their accomplishments and are not afraid to throw themselves into challenging situations. It has been wonderful to have so many positive relationships with women. Reality TV tells us that two women can't be in a room together without calling each other names, fighting, throwing things, or being fake. That is not real life, and it is not cute to consider every other woman an enemy. It is great to have other women to ask questions and to turn to for support. I don't go into situations looking at other women as competition. I do my own thing, let them do theirs, and choose to be friendly even if they are standoffish.

Dealing with Mean People and Bullies

Even though I have that attitude, every woman won't be friendly. I have come across a couple of women who clearly see other women as threats. Often, people who feel threatened lash out. One woman on air who I worked with when I first started on TV would make sly comments about the way I dressed, and another news personality who I met when I was interning never took the conversation beyond "hello" despite my repeated offers to help her with anything she was working on. I am happy to say those instances do not represent the majority of my experiences.

In those cases, I take the treatment as a compliment. There is a reason someone feels threatened by me. In most cases, I just ignored it and didn't make an effort to associate with the person. But if things got to a level where I felt disrespected, I would loudly make a comment on their remarks so that everyone could hear. There is no reason to put up with rude or demeaning behavior from anyone, even if they are in a position higher than you.

The Double Standard

Of course, there are double standards for men and women in society, and the superficial TV industry highlights the different expectations that men and women face. Women are picked apart because of their hair, outfits, and makeup. These are things that viewers hardly ever comment on when it comes to men on TV. If a woman gains a few pounds, there are pregnancy rumors. If a man on TV does, there is usually no mention of his newfound potbelly. I knew that women were more harshly judged by their looks, but now that I am in the news industry, I am reminded of it constantly. There are overwhelmingly more comments on my looks than the content of my interviews. If someone tells me they love watching me, it is often because they think I am attractive. Many times, there is no mention of me being good at what I do.

I find that some men in the industry try to make women feel bad for being judged on their looks, even when it is something we have no control over. Only now, at almost thirty, am I confident enough to speak up for myself and shut these men down. I went to the National Association of Black Journalists conference for the first time in 2014, and I didn't have that confidence yet. It was in Boston, and the conference is a huge deal in the industry. Everyone was telling me that it was great for networking, and that I could get some insightful feedback on my work. I put a video together with some of my recent interviews and news stories and nervously brought it to an area where news managers were reviewing reels and critiquing them.

I spoke to a news manager at a major network who suggested that I read a book called *It Takes More Than Good Looks to Succeed at TV News Reporting.* Maybe he was also suggesting the read to young men in the industry, but by the tone of the conversation, I felt that he was trying to enlighten me to the fact that I would have to do more than look good to be successful in news. I was pissed, but I didn't say anything. I just smiled. I am the first one to scream to young women to not depend on their looks. I pushed my feelings aside, gave the man the benefit of the doubt, and read the book. It did have some helpful information for journalists when it comes to storytelling, but the title is terrible for two reasons. One, there are people making a decent living in the news industry who many could argue are doing way better than more hardworking and qualified people simply because of their looks. The second reason the title rubs me the wrong way is because usually only women are judged by their appearance on TV. The women are often expected to be extraordinarily attractive (even though it's an unspoken expectation), and many men in TV news look like the average guy walking the street. A man wrote the book, and I just felt like it was taking a dig at women who quite frankly are repeatedly shown that they do need good looks to succeed as a reporter.

I went to another news manager who worked in one of the top ten news markets in the country. I was excited to see what he had to say about my work. He appeared to be in his late thirties or early forties, younger than most news directors. He asked me about myself and then randomly shared that he had a reputation for sleeping with all of his talent. Cue the awkward silence. His comments were completely inappropriate and off topic. My older, more confident self would not have been silent. I would question him about the relevance of his statement. I would ask him if he would have made the same comment to a male journalist sitting in front of him. I would not have let him make me feel awkward. I would have turned the energy that he sent out back on him.

I am learning to not just accept the double standards and keep it moving. We, as women, need to constantly remind both men and women how wrong it is to treat women differently than men. Men aren't the only problem. Many women have fallen into the trap too. Lots of women send me mean comments about my hair or outfits, but then finish it off with a statement suggesting that society forced them to make the comment. One time a woman stopped me in the mall after I had worn a natural hairstyle on TV to say, "Girl, you know *we* [black women] can't wear our hair like that." Another will write in, "Your dress was too tight. You don't want to send the wrong message." Ladies, we have to fight back when society tells us to judge other women by the way we look. We have to stop falling into the trap of putting each other into boxes based on how we wear our hair or clothing. We have to stop believing that we have to accept that we will be judged by our looks. We can change the standard. We can call people out for their inappropriate and rude behavior each and every time it happens.

Being a woman in such a superficial industry has its added challenges, but instead of bending to these challenges and feeling bad about myself or the way I look, I am more determined to encourage people to look beyond appearance. I am not delusional. Humans are visual creatures. It is natural to process whether we find someone attractive or not on first glance, but can we leave it at that and not decide whether a woman is good at her job based on superficial factors? Hopefully, one day the answer will be a resounding yes.

18
Paying It Forward

When you learn, teach. When you get, give.

Maya Angelou

Becoming a Mentor

A big part of the reason I am in the news industry is because Soledad and Kim mentored me and helped me finish college. Soledad and Kim continue to open the door to more opportunities for me. In the fall of 2016, Soledad helped me make my national television debut. She was working on a PBS special called *American Graduate Day*, and through my connection with her, I got the job of doing the live interviews for the show. PBS flew me in, and I was live on the streets of New York City for the nation to watch. Soledad flies me all over the country to emcee PowHERful Foundation events. It is great to be able to tell young women that I was in their shoes just a few years ago. Soledad has also set me up with some great interviews at her events. I interviewed celebrities such as Pharrell Williams, Iyanla Vanzant, and Tatyana Ali at events with Soledad.

Soledad has provided amazing opportunities for many other girls through her PowHERful Foundation. Things certainly come full circle, because I am now a mentor with her organization. I am flattered that many young girls ask me to mentor them, but right now, I have only one mentee, mainly because I want to be available to her.

I was hesitant about being a mentor. When PowHERful asked me to mentor Tassion, a freshman at Dillard University who was interested in journalism, I didn't know if I was the best choice for her. I was still living at home, in tons of debt, and seeking guidance from my mentors all the time.

Kim and Soledad assured me that I was ready to be a mentor. After giving it some thought, I realized that my inexperience and the struggles I was going through would only give me more lessons to pass along to her as I navigated through them. I thought about who I would want insight from if I needed a route around a closed bridge: I would want to ask the person who just crossed, as opposed to the person who crossed thirty years ago. The latter person is far past that bridge now and in a great place professionally, but they barely remember crossing that one little bridge—for instance, choosing a college major. It's a huge hurdle when you're in the process of doing it. I have been out of college for only a few years, so those college struggles and the immediate aftermath are still very fresh to me. Tassion and I spend a lot of time together, and when I doubt my mentoring skills, she always assures me that I am a great help to her.

It is never too early to start helping someone who is coming up behind you. There are so many things that I have experienced that I don't even think about until Tassion tells me a story, and I realize that I have been through a similar situation. Often, the way I dealt with the situation can be helpful to her or sometimes it is simply reassuring for her to know I went though a similar phase. For instance, Tassion is still trying to figure out her career path, but whenever she stresses about it, I remind her that I changed my educational focus several times and had no idea what I would be doing until I was a senior in college. I had to reframe the way I was thinking about mentoring. A fifth grader can help a fourth grader with homework. It's not about age. It is about patience and openness. I can't help someone if I am not willing to be honest about how I got to where I am. Imagine you and a friend are both saving for a house. You talk about how difficult it is. You both have similar incomes. Then she buys a house two years before you do, but she never mentioned that her parents gave her the down payment for a house. Her advice is going to be pretty useless to you if she is leaving out the most important thing: the down payment. I have to be honest about my journey to help others.

These days, everything is about image. People don't want to water down their dreams with the truth, but the truth is very humbling to me. I couldn't be where I am today without the help of a lot of people. And even with their help, there will always be parts of my story that shouldn't have aligned but did. I don't know why things worked out so that I was able to graduate from college without ever saving a dime for it. I will never be able to explain how I ended up in news and found so many opportunities for advancement—and right in my hometown. All of these inexplicable parts of my story remind me that there is a higher power, which is beyond my control.

How I Mentor

When I finally decided that I would take the leap and become a mentor, I was worried that I didn't know how to mentor. The first time Tassion and I

Soledad O'Brien's PowHERful Foundation event in New Orleans, with my mentee, Tassion Minor. (Photograph by author)

The 2016 PowHERful Foundation gala in New York, with my mentee, Tassion Minor (left), and Kim Bondy (center). (Photograph by author)

met up officially, we chatted at a coffee shop. I stopped stressing so much and thought about how Kim mentored me. I invited Tassion to shadow me at work and to come to cool events where I emceed or spoke. Sometimes, she just comes over and hangs out, and other times, we go out to eat. She is already like my little sister. We talk about school, our families, and what she wants to do with her life. She thinks that she wants to be a journalist, and it has been amazing to share with her what I have learned in my journey.

Helping Everyone

I get emails and calls from people telling me how they or their children look up to me. I don't like to call myself a role model because I don't do things to purposefully set a good example. Usually, my motivation for doing something is because it makes me happy or will help me grow in some way. If I were to declare myself a role model, then I feel I would have to think of others first when I do things, and that's just not the way I want to live my life. I am very aware, though, that some young women do look up to me, and I take that very seriously. However, I will never choose not to do something because it's not considered role model behavior. If I want to wear short shorts, I am going to wear them. I am going to be me regardless, and I want young girls who look up to me to be encouraged to be themselves too.

Paying it forward lies at the core of my brand. The further along I get in my career, the more I want to help others, especially those who look up to me. Part of my inspiration for sharing my story is that I think someone else might be able to relate to it. I have started a blog, called *Off Air*, where I share even more of my life behind the scenes, to show people what I am really going through. I also interview other people about their journeys to success and all of the struggles that came along the way. I find new ways to pay it forward every day. It may be just responding to an email from an aspiring journalist. Sometimes, I invite aspiring journalists to shadow me for a day at work. I also help my new coworkers navigate some of the newbie mistakes I made. I want to be someone who helps others. The more I am blessed and awarded opportunities, the bigger my ability to pass those blessings on to others. I am happy when I know that someone worries a little less or feels more inspired because of me. I do believe that happiness is contagious, and I find power in spreading it to other people.

19
Success?

*If you look to others for fulfillment, you will never be
fulfilled. If your happiness depends on money, you will
never be happy with yourself. Be content with what you
have; rejoice in the way things are. When you realize
there is nothing lacking, the world belongs to you.*

Lao-tzu

As I finish this book, I have come to the end of my three-year contract as
an anchor with WWL. Now, I am so much more comfortable at the anchor
desk and in the field than I was three years ago, but now it's time to be
uncomfortable again. Because of the nature of contracts for on-air talent,
every few years of my life will be like a new beginning. I will have to reevaluate
what I want for myself and my career. I will have to reconsider which city I
want to work in and wait to hear if the station I work for wants to keep me.
What am I worth to them, now that I have been in the business for a few
years and have shown what I am capable of doing? And how do I stand up for
myself in negotiations and make sure that I get what I am worth?

Thankfully, I am not alone. I had the opportunity—while speaking at
Soledad's 2017 annual gala for PowHERful Foundation—to meet her agent,
who just happened to be there. He was impressed with my speech, introduced
himself, and told me that while he usually wouldn't be interested in someone
at my career level, he saw something special in me. It was perfect timing. I
needed someone experienced in my corner, someone who could help me
negotiate and shape my career goals. Just like that, I had a team of agents at
one of the world's largest talent agencies in New York on my side. And yet the
process of making the next step into my future is still not easy.

As I try to figure out my next move, I also feel the old "yes girl"—the girl who
says "okay" and "yes" to everything to avoid any sort of confrontation—creeping

up out of me. That attitude certainly is not going to work in negotiations, because even with my agents, I have to be assertive about what I want them to get for me. I also struggle with valuing myself. How do I yell to the world that I know I am good at what I do, that I work hard, that I am an asset to a news station without sounding cocky? How do I show that I am grateful but ask for more? And what exactly should my next move be?

I love *The Wendy Williams Show*. Her show is always lighthearted, fun, and entertaining, and I admire that she doesn't take herself or her show too seriously. It's pretty impossible not to love Ellen DeGeneres. Her show is really fun too, and she always keeps things positive and inspiring. And then my old favorite was *The Tyra Banks Show*. She tackled a range of serious to lighthearted topics and always had some great conversations. My ultimate vision is to have my own national daytime talk show like Wendy or Ellen or Tyra, but when people ask about my vision for the next five or ten years, I don't have any answer besides, eventually, landing that talk show. Hosting a talk show is a not a career that comes with a step-by-step guide to exactly how to get there.

Some days I still feel like a little girl who doesn't know how to answer when people ask "What do you want to be when you grow up?" I haven't discovered my purpose yet in life. I like my job, but purpose is bigger than that. It's about what I am meant to do while I am here on the earth. I believe our passions help us find our purpose. I like being on TV, but it is not my passion or purpose. It is simply the medium through which I tell stories.

When I was younger, I looked at a successful career as an end point. I thought there'd be a moment when I'd get to say, "Whew, I'm an anchor now. I can relax and coast from here!" Success is proving to be a constant journey towards getting better. Once I made it to the anchor desk, that old feeling of being an outsider came back again. There were so many words I didn't know, so many things that seemed basic to everyone else but that I had never heard of. Sometimes, I still don't feel like I am in the right place because I don't know enough or haven't been exposed to enough. But I always go back to my way of coping in elementary school. The right amount of preparation can make up for a lack of natural abilities. I have reached my original end goal, and now I am setting new goals.

On the financial front, all $60,000 of that student loan debt is gone. It took a lot of deprivation and discipline to get it done. I kept my "struggle car" until I reached my goal. I just recently bought another car. Now, it's time to tackle new financial goals and set myself up to be financially stable for the rest of my life. It is not easy. I am still working to make a budget and stick with it. I want to learn more about the stock market. I am looking into the financial freedom that real estate can provide. There are tons of financial goals on my to-do list for life, and sometimes I am overwhelmed and frustrated by my lack of financial knowledge. But I ask questions, pick up a book, or get on the internet, and I get to work. I know that one day I will be exactly where I want to be financially, and I'll smile at the old Sheba who was trying to figure it all out.

My definition of success has evolved over the years. I badly wanted to be hired at our competing station, WDSU, when I finished interning. Remember that manager who shook his head when I was an intern and someone who worked at the station suggested I go cover a story? He eventually reached out to talk to me about working at WDSU, but by then I was advancing at WWL and realized that I was in the exact place I was supposed to be. At one point, I wanted nothing more than to be hired by WDSU. When I didn't get a job there, it was a huge disappointment at the time. By the time that manager reached out, I had outgrown that dream. Once again, something that seemed to be a letdown turned out to be a setup for an even better opportunity. My idea of success used to be as simple as landing a good job, having a solid paycheck, getting my finances together, and living in a certain city. Then, I realized just getting a paycheck wasn't enough. I wanted a paycheck from doing something meaningful and fulfilling. Soledad and Kim showed me that a big part of being successful is being able to give back. And I realized very quickly that without happiness, success is meaningless. My mom always told me that I had to be happy when I was alone in bed by myself at the end of the day. It has been a good exercise to keep me focused on what I want and has helped me not get trapped by what society says will make me happy.

Many people ask me whether I want to stay in New Orleans or work in a bigger market, and it's a tricky question to answer because I have learned that happiness and success are not defined by the city I live in or the company I work for. My plan was to leave New Orleans. I figured that after I had worked at the job in Lafayette, I would move to somewhere else in the country. When I first met Soledad, people assumed I was chasing after a job in New York. But I wanted to report, and there are hardly any opportunities for someone with no experience to report in New York. So far, New Orleans has held the best opportunities for me, so this is where I am. I have learned to chase opportunity, not specific cities or job titles.

We are taught to think about what our perfect partner looks like, but it's also important to think about what the perfect version of ourselves looks like. Then, figure out what it takes to create that vision and get to work. When I was at the National Association of Black Journalists conference in Boston not long after I signed my first anchor contract, another executive at a major network basically told me my journey was going all wrong. Yeah, I didn't have the best time there. This man suggested I demote myself from *The 504* and the anchor desk, because it happened too soon for me. He said I would benefit more from being a reporter for a longer period of time.

At first, he made me feel bad. And then I remembered that people can tell you only what they know. Maybe that's what every success story he knows of looks like, and that's ok. I have grown to be confident in accepting my journey and how it differs from everyone else, and I celebrate and fully embrace that difference. It is *my* journey. No one else has to understand it.

I don't even understand it, and I now embrace that uncertainty as part of my journey. I used to think of a detour as something negative, as something that was getting me off track. My life has shown me that sometimes we are off track and don't even know it. Many times, those things that we think are detours are actually setting us on the path that is destined for us. I constantly felt like I was being thrown off track as I tried to set myself up for a successful future. I was confused about which career path to pursue in college, and I couldn't even figure out how to pay for school. Without those detours, I would not have ended up in news. I needed to be confused because that forced me to explore options outside of the medical field, which I was on the path to enter. If I would not have run out of money for college, I never would have met Kim and Soledad after enrolling at the University of New Orleans.

Going through some disappointment has given me a lot of perspective, but that perspective is not a cure-all. I still feel confusion, doubt, anxiety, worry, and all those other emotions that come along with the rollercoaster ride that is life. But when I step away from those feelings to assess what I am going through and what I should do, I have a sense of calm that I did not have when I was younger. I now trust that everything that is happening has a purpose. The bad moments are part of the journey too. I can't wish them away because without them I cannot fulfill my destiny. I used to freak out about not knowing exactly what I want to do with my life, but now I realize that maybe I am not supposed to know yet. When it is time for me to move onto the next phase of my purpose, it will be revealed to me. In the meantime, I enjoy the ride and focus on working hard.

One of the most eye-opening revelations of my career has been that hard work isn't enough. There are many hard-working people who are not where they want to be. It isn't enough just to work hard, I have to be strategic and progress toward specific goals. As long as I keep moving forward, it is inevitable that I will run into new opportunities. I didn't grow up in an environment that screamed success, but education helped bridge the gap between my present and my future. Every time I got derailed, I had to keep moving until things started making sense again. Having people who were there when things got tough made a world of difference for me, and I will forever be indebted to everyone who took the time to help, encourage, and support me along my journey. I also find comfort in seeing how strong I am. I know that I would not have made it here if I had not stayed focused. I know now that I really can do anything, not because of luck or magic, but because I will decide to do it and will do whatever it takes to get it done.

When I set a goal, I take the first small step toward it—and then another and then another, and eventually, I will get there. And when, finally, it all starts to go even better than I planned, I embrace it and enjoy the little moments. I have decided not to wait until I have reached some end goal to be happy, because it might not happen. That's just life. But the moment I am in right now—I have that. It is mine. So I own it and enjoy it as I push toward even bigger goals. To some, it seems I already have a storybook ending. Off air, the work is just beginning.